NON-FICTION TO 14

ANSWER BOOK

JENNY ROBERTS

OXFORD
UNIVERSITY PRESS

OXFORD
UNIVERSITY PRESS

Great Clarendon Street, Oxford, OX2 6DP, United Kingdom

Oxford University Press is a department of the University of Oxford. It furthers the University's objective of excellence in research, scholarship, and education by publishing worldwide. Oxford is a registered trade mark of Oxford University Press in the UK and in certain other countries

First published in 2018

British Library Cataloguing in Publication Data

Data available

ISBN 978-0-19-837684-2

10 9 8 7 6 5 4 3 2 1

Printed in Great Britain by CPI Group (UK) Ltd., Croydon CR0 4YY

Acknowledgements

The author and publisher are grateful for permission to reprint extracts from the following copyright material:

Tanya Basu: 'Something called "attention residue" is ruining your concentration', *New York Magazine* - 'Science of Us', 21 Jan 2016, reprinted by permission of New York Media.

Luke Brown: 'The kitesurfer who defied a coma', *Daily Telegraph*, 26 April 2016, copyright © Telegraph Media Group Ltd 2016, reprinted by permission of TMG.

Roger Callan: 'Would you like to sit on the floor?', *The Independent*, 7 April 1999, copyright © The Independent 1999, reprinted by permission of Independent Print Ltd/ ESI Media.

Richard Feynman: *Surely You're Joking Mr Feynman: adventures of a curious character as told to Ralph Leighton* (Vintage 1992), copyright © Richard Feynman 1985, 1992, reprinted by permission of The Random House Group Ltd

Josh Gardner: 'Hotel unveils ROBOT butler that makes automated room service calls and accepts reviews from guests instead of tips' *Mailonline*, 12 Aug 2014, copyright © Associated Newspapers Ltd 2014, reprinted by permission of Solo Syndication

The Guardian Archive: Review - Theatre Royal *Richard III*, 3 Sept 1825; 'Londoners skate on thin ice', 23 Dec 1864; and 'The servantless house', 28 Dec 1921; copyright © Guardian News & Media Ltd 2017, reprinted by permission of GNM.

James Harrison: 'The Foodbank dilemma', *New Statesman*, October 2014, copyright © New Statesman 2014, reprinted by permission of New Statesman.

C S Lewis: Letter to Joan Lancaster, 1956, from *C S Lewis' Letters to Children* (Collins, 1985, copyright © C S Lewis Pte Ltd 1985, reprinted by permission of The C S Lewis Company Ltd.

Alyson Lynch: 'Penguin swims 5000 miles every year for reunion with man who saved his life', *Metro*, 9 March 2016, copyright © Associated Newspapers Ltd 2016, reprinted by permission of Solo Syndication.

Robert Macfarlane: *The Old Ways: a journey on foot* (Penguin, 2013), copyright © Robert Macfarlane 2013, reprinted by permission of Penguin Books Ltd.

George Orwell: *Down and Out in Paris and London* (Penguin, 2013), copyright © George Orwell 1933, reprinted by permission of A M Heath & Co Ltd, on behalf of the Estate of George Orwell.

Sue Townsend: 'A Passion for Books', copyright © Sue Townsend 1992, in *The Pleasure of Reading* edited by Antonia Fraser (Bloomsbury, 1992), reprinted by permission of Curtis Brown Group Ltd, London on behalf of the Estate of Sue Townsend

Peter Travers: Review of William Shakespeare's *Romeo and Juliet*, *Rolling Stone Magazine*, 1 Nov 1996, copyright © Rolling Stone LLC 1996, reprinted by permission of Rolling Stone LLC. All rights reserved.

Alfred Wainwright: *The Southern Fells* (Frances Lincoln, 2005), *Pictorial Guides to the Lakelands*, Book 4, copyright © The Estate of A Wainright 1960, reprinted by permission of Frances Lincoln Ltd, Quarto Publishing plc.

David Walliams: 'Roald Dahl and Me', *The Independent*, 4 Nov 2009, copyright © The Independent 2009, reprinted by permission of Independent Print Ltd/ ESI Media.

Jacqueline Wilson: 'Top Tips for Creative Writing', 17 March 2017, W H Smith blog, reprinted by permission of David Higham Associates.

Although we have made every effort to trace and contact all copyright holders before publication this has not been possible in all cases. If notified, the publisher will rectify any errors or omissions at the earliest opportunity.

The publisher and authors would like to thank the following for permission to use photographs and other copyright material:

Cover: sharpstock/Alamy Stock Photo; Vera Holera/Shutterstock;

Every effort has been made to contact copyright holders of material reproduced in this book. Any omissions will be rectified in subsequent printings if notice is given to the publisher.

Contents

Welcome to *Non-Fiction To 14*. We know from talking to lots of English teachers that you have been wanting a resource that helps build students' understanding of a wider range of texts – in particular, non-fiction texts. Well, here it is.

In putting *Non-Fiction To 14* together, we wanted to achieve a number of aims. First, we wanted to serve up an eclectic range of writing, genres and styles that would surprise and entertain students. You'll find an extraordinary variety of sources here including essays, letters, reviews, blogs, speeches, journal entries, newspaper and magazine articles, biography, travel writing and guides all of which have been carefully selected to interest and engage students.

We also wanted to provide a rich range of texts written across different time periods because we know that students need to build their confidence with the language and stylistic conventions of 19th-, 20th- and 21st-century texts. This is also an essential way of building students' reading resilience, that ability to enjoy rather than be scared of encountering the unfamiliar.

The activities throughout the book have been written to develop the skills students need to read and respond to non-fiction texts, from comprehension skills, to analysing how language and structure can be used to convey meaning and create deliberate effects. Additional activities help students make comparisons across and between texts, further developing their critical reading skills.

As well as developing students' skills as critical readers of non-fiction texts, specific activities are designed to nurture their abilities as writers, enabling them to draw on the techniques they have explored in their reading when writing themselves.

This *Answer Book* includes both questions and sample answers for the activities in the *Student Book*. With these, we are not of course suggesting that only one answer will fit, but experience tells us that students need to learn that in English it's all about how we express our ideas as well as what we say. The sample answers are designed to help encourage students towards an appropriate style. I hope you will find them helpful and that the suggested answers will help with your own evaluation of your students' progress.

Geoff Barton

1.1 'The kitesurfer who defied a coma' by Luke Brown, 2016

Basic reading skills

1 **Look again at the opening paragraph of the article. Write down three facts we learn about Lewis Crathern.**

He is a kitesurfer; he had a crash three months ago; he was in a coma in a South African hospital.

2 **In the second paragraph, the writer explains what led to Lewis Crathern's accident. He says he was attempting a 'routine kite loop'. What does the word 'routine' mean in this context?**

An activity that he often did

3 **Look at the third paragraph. Lewis Crathern is competing 'off the picture-postcard coast of El Gouna'. Which of the terms below is closest in meaning to 'picture-postcard'? Write it down and explain your answer in a sentence.**

Beautiful. The coast is so beautiful that it might feature on the front of a postcard that people buy to send to their friends or keep as a souvenir.

4 **As well as being a successful kitesurfer, what two roles is Lewis Crathern known for back home?**

Commentator and public speaker

5 **Why is Egypt popular with kitesurfers?**

It offers ideal conditions in which to practise.

6 **At the start and end of the article, Lewis Crathern says that kitesurfing is a safe sport. Write down one reason that he gives.**

People receive a much better 'introduction' to the sport, meaning training.

Advanced reading skills

1 **Look at the opening sentence. How does the writer draw the reader into the article?**

The quotation is a strong, simple statement, but also seemingly contradictory (kitesurfing conjures up an image of a dangerous, dramatic, high-intensity sport), so the readers' curiosity is aroused and they want to read on.

2 **Throughout the article the writer refers to his subject as 'Crathern', not as 'Lewis Crathern' or just 'Lewis'. In your own words explain what effect this has and how the article would be different if the writer used the first name Lewis throughout.**

The use of his surname makes the reference more formal, implying that he is a professional who the author respects, rather than a friend. The use of his first name would be less formal and more personal; it would imply the focus was more on the man himself than his role as a competitor.

3 **In the third paragraph the writer uses the phrase 'gloriously understated fashion'. Explain what you think 'gloriously' means in this context.**

Hugely and humorously

4 **In the sixth paragraph, the writer describes Crathern as 'a man whose lifestyle appears almost as extreme as the profession he lives for'. In your own words, explain what you think he means.**

The way Crathern lives his life – travelling the world, being extremely busy, striving for success and taking on challenges – echoes the intensity with which he participates in his sport.

5 **In the ninth paragraph, Lewis Crathern describes the accident he had in South Africa. Choose two words from the list below that you think best describe his attitude. Explain your choices.**

Unconcerned and blasé. He does not dwell on what went wrong and does not fear future accidents. He accepts that he was 'unlucky' and seems convinced that the sport is genuinely safe and that accidents can happen anywhere to anyone, even if they aren't taking part in an extreme sport.

6 **How does the writer present Lewis Crathern? Does he seem to view him completely as a hero, or does he seem to have some criticisms of him? Write a paragraph in which you discuss the way the subject is presented.**

Sample answer

The writer presents Lewis Crathern as someone who has many admirable qualities, such as being a successful sportsman (he has a 'formidable kitesurfing CV') and 'one of sport's biggest personalities' as a speaker and commentator. He also seems to admire his resilience and energy, describing his lifestyle 'as extreme as the profession he lives for'. However, there is also a suggestion that Crathern is slightly deluded about the risks he takes and the risks associated with the sport. The writer can't quite take his opinions seriously, 'you could be forgiven for thinking he is joking', and describes some of his comments as 'gloriously understated'. The writer also notes how amazed Crathern is that his crash had such an impact on his family. This suggests that Crathern isn't particularly sensitive to how other people feel. His insistence about the safety of the sport is slightly questioned by the writer's description of the way he 'pointedly reiterates' this view. It is almost as if he is saying it too much, as if desperate to convince others, and perhaps also himself.

1.2 'Flying the English Channel' by Harriet Quimby, 1912

Basic reading skills

1a Re-read the opening paragraph. At what time does Harriet Quimby take off?

5.30 in the morning

1b How long does it take Harriet Quimby to reach a height of 1500 feet?

30 seconds

1c What landmark has Harriet Quimby promised the photographers she would fly towards after take-off?

The flagpole of Dover Castle

2a What are the weather conditions like during Harriet Quimby's crossing of the channel? Pick out two quotations that you think best show this.

'the quickening fog obscured my view'; 'the wind had risen and the currents were coming in billowy gusts'

2b List two actions that Harriet Quimby takes to cope with the effects of the weather conditions.

She keeps her eye on her compass because of the fog. She pushes her goggles up onto her forehead because she can't see out of them due to the damp.

3 Name the two places where Harriet Quimby could land when she reaches France. Explain which one she chooses and why.

She could land on the farmers' fields or on the beach. She chooses the beach so as not to damage the farmland.

4 Who are the first people to know that Harriet Quimby has successfully crossed the English Channel?

A crowd of men, women and children who were fishing

Advanced reading skills

1 How does the writer's use of prepositional phrases help the reader to share her experience?

Sample answer

She uses prepositional phrases to give the reader a very definite sense of time and location as she recounts her experience, for example, 'In a moment', 'in a long circle', 'within thirty seconds', 'In an instant', 'until I was half that height', 'on which to alight', 'from my machine', 'from all directions'.

2 Re-read the paragraph beginning: 'My hands were covered with long Scotch woolen gloves...'. Comment on how the writer's use of sentence forms conveys Harriet Quimby's feelings and actions. You should comment on the effects created by the variety of sentence types, for example, single and multi-clause.

Sample answer

This paragraph opens with multi-clause sentences which contain statements and then continues with explanations or descriptions of effects. This conveys the impression of the pilot dealing with an ongoing situation as she flies along. The short statement 'I could not see through them' is quite abrupt, and slightly shocking, echoing the realization that she is in danger. This is further built upon by the next statement about her speed, and conveys the feeling of tension and drama. The following multi-clause sentence describes her reflections about distance and the next explains her consequent action. The shorter, simpler sentence 'I felt happy, but could not find Calais' reflects her burst of positive feeling, closely followed by alarm. The final sentence is long, containing three clauses, echoing her clear, decisive reaction to the situation.

3 **Compare this autobiographical account with the newspaper article on pages 14–15. What impression do you get of Harriet Quimby's and Lewis Crathern's achievements?**

Sample answer

Both accounts focus on people who take on dangerous challenges and are determined to achieve success. Both Quimby and Crathern seem to be competitive by nature. Quimby describes the excitement of the fishermen who recognize that she is 'the first woman' to cross the channel by aeroplane, and Crathern is obviously determined to compete and win in his sport. Both Quimby and Crathern seem very focused on their challenges, and keen to tackle them with minimum fuss. Before Quimby's flight we are told that 'preliminaries were brief' and Crathern is determined to play down the dangerous aspects of kitesurfing.

Both Quimby and Crathern seem to have clear analytical minds that can read the situation they are in very speedily and sensibly without undue emotion. Both seem to react quickly to problems with constructive solutions and don't dwell on possible negative outcomes.

The writer of the article about Crathern seems to cast a few doubts about how realistic Crathern's attitude is. There is a suggestion that he is in denial about the dangers he faces and minimizes the risks involved in the sport, so the reader is left with an impression of a slightly reckless sportsman. The extract about Quimby is autobiographical, so we get a clear insight into her thoughts and feelings, all of which seem admirably intelligent and measured. There is no denial of the dangers she faces, but she concentrates on overcoming them.

1.3 'Londoners skate on thin ice', 1874

Basic reading skills

1a **How many people fell into the water when skating on the frozen lake in Regent's Park?**

20

1b **How many people in total does the writer say went skating on the Long Water in Kensington Gardens?**

1500

1c **Were the people who went skating in St James's Park mainly male or female?**

Male (boys)

2 **What was the young man who drowned in the Serpentine heard to say before he went skating on the lake?**

'I'll put on my skates and prove it all right.'

3a **Pick out a quotation that shows the first attempt to rescue the man drowning in the Serpentine was unsuccessful.**

'their efforts were futile'

3b **Explain your choice of quotation, commenting on any specific words that convey the failure of the rescue attempt.**

'Futile' means ineffective and pointless, which shows that the efforts to save the drowning man failed.

4 **The writer begins the final paragraph: 'After this another tragical scene occurred...'. Explain whether you agree that the scene described in this paragraph is a 'tragical' one. Give reasons for your answer.**

Sample answer

I don't think that this scene is really 'tragical' because the men who had been swimming in the water did survive, after being given warm baths and 'stimulants'. It would have been more tragic if they had died too.

Advanced reading skills

1 **How does the writer convey the risk of skating on London's frozen lakes?**

Sample answer

The writer conveys the risk of skating on London's frozen lakes by describing the 'dangerous state of the ice', thereby flagging up the danger that they voluntarily embrace. The title of the article, 'skating on thin ice', is clever because it not only describes what actually happened but this is also a phrase that is used to describe anything that is potentially dangerous or precarious. The writer points out that William Hemmings, the rescuer of four men, acted 'at the risk of his own life', suggesting that the original skaters were rather foolish to expose themselves to danger, forcing someone else into danger in order to rescue them. The young man's boasting that he will 'prove it all right' is ironic, in that he ultimately proved that the ice was not all right, and it claimed his life.

2 **Look again at the three paragraphs describing the rescue of the drowning man from the Serpentine, beginning 'His friends' cries for help were appalling...'.**

How does the writer's use of language help to build tension in this section?

Sample answer

The writer's choice of vocabulary helps to build the tension in this extract. The description of the cries for help being 'appalling' conveys the impression of desperation and panic among the drowning man's friends. The builder who tries the first rescue is described as 'a fine young fellow', suggesting a typical heroic character, who didn't hesitate to shed his coat before he 'plunged in'. The naming of the other three men who joined the rescue and the description of the floating ice are contained in a long multi-clause sentence, which delays the reader from knowing the outcome. The news that their efforts were in vain ('futile') comes at the very end of the paragraph.

The next paragraph continues the saga, using a long, multi-clause sentence to prolong the suspense of the narrative. The eventual mention of 'the lifeless body' being 'drawn out of the water' conjures up a vivid image of the scene. The focus on the body is a stark reminder that the energy and personality of the man himself was gone, and only his corpse remained.

3 **Read what the following student has written about this text:**

I think if this newspaper article was written today it would be a lot more sensationalized.

Explain what you think this student means and then say whether you agree or disagree with the statement. Give reasons for your answer.

Sample answer

I think this student means that today news articles often try and stir up a lot more emotion in the reader, so that they react more intensely to a news report. I agree with this statement because nowadays the media has to compete for people's attention as we are surrounded by so many different sources of information, such as TV, radio, online news reports, social media and so on. Today, the report might focus more on how irresponsible the skaters were, rather than just imply it. It might also give more gory details about the body, and exaggerate the rescue attempts, making them seem even more heroic and memorable. The description of the people floundering in the water would probably be drawn out more, including some eyewitness quotations that focus on the terror demonstrated by those who had fallen in. There would also probably be some mention of lack of health and safety rules, who might be responsible and might be sued, and also the long-term traumatic effects on those who had fallen in, those who attempted rescues and those who witnessed any of the scenes.

2.1 'Something Called "Attention Residue" Is Ruining Your Concentration' by Tanya Basu, 2016

Basic reading skills

1 **Look again at the first paragraph. Give three examples of things that the writer lists as potential distractions.**

Eating lunch; reading the latest news about what Donald Trump has said; sending out a few memos.

2 **What is the title of Professor Cal Newport's new book?**

Deep Work: Rules for Focused Success in a Distracted World

3 **The writer states that Professor Newport's book 'attempts to understand how workers can rise above their infomania'.**

a Using information from the blog, provide definitions for the following terms.

- **infomania** – the desire to access information from different sources the whole time
- **time-crunched** – time is squeezed and compressed as people try to fit more into less time
- **attention residue** – thoughts and concentration from one task that is still lingering when working on the next task
- **deep work** – intense focus on a single activity

b Using your own words, explain what Professor Newport's book is trying to help workers to do.

To maximize their productivity by focusing on doing one thing at a time, rather than by trying to multitask and change activities before one has been completed thoroughly.

4a **Did Sophie Leroy's 2009 study find that people were more or less productive when switching between different tasks?**

Less productive

4b **Using your own words, explain why Sophie Leroy thought this was.**

Sample answer

Leroy thought that unless people finished one task before starting another they would still have part of their mind focused on the previous task when starting the new one, so they don't concentrate fully and work less productively.

5 **Look again at the final paragraph. Summarize the advice this gives.**

Just focus on one task at a time and don't let anything else distract you until you complete that particular task.

Advanced reading skills

1 **A blog post is designed to be read online and has to compete for a reader's attention with other articles and tasks. How does the language that Tanya Basu uses help to attract and maintain the reader's attention?**

Sample answer

The writer uses the second person to address the reader directly, as 'you'. This creates the effect of a very direct personal approach, which it would be impolite to ignore. The language style is conversational, for example, the repeated use of 'but', and the reflective tone of 'well' and the rhetorical question 'right?' This tone feels intimate and chatty, like a friendly voice. Some phrases are very informal, for example, 'banging out that presentation', 'gets nods' and 'on the right foot', again reinforcing the sense of friendly, sympathetic advice. Towards the end of the passage, some statements are very short and truncated, for example, 'Most important' followed by an imperative 'Don't stop...'. This gives the impression of short, sharp advice that needs to be listened to. It gives the message authority and conveys the message simply and clearly.

2 **Look again at the paragraph beginning, '[P]eople need to stop thinking about one task...'.**

a How formal is the register of language used here? Support your answer with reference to the text.

The writing becomes more impersonal and more formal as this paragraph makes some important statements which are at the root of the whole argument. The use of the word 'people' shows that the advice is relevant to all people, not just one individual. It is a global statement of fact and sounds authoritative.

b Does the informality of the language in the rest of the text influence your response to the idea presented? Explain why.

The informal language helps to catch and retain the reader's attention but the more formal parts present most of the facts, issues and advice. The combination of informal and formal language makes the reader respond to the blog positively, aware that the advice is valuable to them as an individual, as well as to people generally.

3 **How does the structure of the blog post help Tanya Basu to present and explore the concept of 'attention residue' and how this can be overcome? Copy and complete the table to identify the focus of each paragraph.**

Paragraph	Focus
1	Gives examples of some of the distractions found in a modern-day workplace, addressed directly to the reader.
2	Introduces the concept of 'attention residue' and mentions the book in which it is explained.
3	Explains the problem people have, needing to switch between tasks, but being less productive as a result.
4	States the fact that for peak productivity, people need to focus on just one task at a time.
5	Explains why 'attention residue' is counterproductive and wastes time.
6	Core advice to finish one task before starting another to work most effectively.

4 **Tanya Basu creates links between paragraphs to help develop the ideas she presents and improve the coherence of the text. Find more examples of the links the writer creates between paragraphs and explore how these links help her to develop ideas and improve the coherence of the text.**

Sample answer

The second paragraph ends with the phrase 'attention residue' and the third paragraph opens by picking up on this phrase with a question about what it is. This third paragraph ends with a colon to introduce the third paragraph which goes into more detail about the theory. In the fourth paragraph, the writer explains more fully the practical implications of the theory, explaining how it works in real life. The paragraph finishes with the statement 'it's actually a time-waster.'

The fifth paragraph picks up on this final idea, saying 'Here's where...', and goes on to explain the solution. Near the end of the final paragraph the writer refers again to the situation when you have a presentation due the next day. This links back to the situation described in the opening paragraph, so completes the logical circular shape of the text.

2.2 *The Young Woman's Book: A Useful Manual for Everyday Life* by Laura Valentine, 1877

Basic reading skills

1a **Look again at the first paragraph. What two adjectives does the writer use to describe a novel?**

Foolish, wise

1b **Pick out the quotation that you think best shows the writer's attitude to reading novels.**

'absolutely wicked'

1c **Summarize why the writer feels this way about reading novels.**

The writer thinks that the lure of novels is evil because it distracts people from their responsibilities and duties.

2 **List three pieces of evidence the writer gives that suggest the mother neglected her children.**

They were dirty, had tatty clothes and weren't taught anything.

3 **What happened to the woman's husband when he came home from sea?**

He went to prison because the woman had run up debts that couldn't be paid.

4 **What happened to the woman's son?**

He ran away from school and disappeared in Australia.

5 **Look again at the following sentence:**

'The daughter, trained only in the unreal folly of novels, married secretly a man much below her father's station – he was also an hereditary madman!'

a Rewrite this sentence in your own words.

Sample answer

The daughter, who only had the example of her mother constantly reading novels, married a man that was poorer and of a lower status than her father and who also had mental health problems.

b Explain what the phrase 'unreal folly of novels' suggests about the writer's attitude to reading novels.

Sample answer

The phrase suggests that novels are not linked to reality – they are unreal or pure escapism. It also suggests that novels are a folly – something artificial and self-indulgent, created on a whim for no practical purpose. The writer obviously sees reading novels as a complete waste of time and a foolish way to indulge one's imagination.

6 **Now look at the final paragraph. What does the writer compare reading a novel to? Explain whether you think this is an appropriate comparison.**

The comparison is with an addiction such as alcohol or drugs, which gives the victim an artificial high but only temporarily, and does long-term damage.

Advanced reading skills

1 **The writer uses hyperbole to present her view of the dangers of novel reading.**

a Pick out any examples of hyperbole you can find in the text.

Reading novels is 'absolutely wicked'; house is 'dirty beyond description'; son is 'utterly ruined'; 'misery on her and on two following generations'

b How effective do you think the writer's use of hyperbole is? Give reasons for your answer.

Sample answer

The use of hyperbole is effective because it conjures up a very dramatic, startling picture of ruined lives, giving the message of the text a strong impact. However, it is so exaggerated that it rather undermines the value of the text because it seems too extreme to be true.

2 **How does the writer use emotive language to present her view of the dangers of novel reading?**

Sample answer

The writer chooses to use language that will stir up the reader's emotions, such as outrage, horror and pity. The choice of words such as 'wicked', 'waste', 'dishonesty' and 'neglected' convey a sense of moral corruption, persuading the reader to believe that reading novels can lead to terrible consequences. The emphasis is not only on the effect on the novel reader, but also on her family which makes her dereliction of duties seem even more selfish. The neglect of children, left 'dirty, ragged, untaught' and running wild, conjures up a disturbing image of feral children having to fend for themselves without support or comfort. The fate of the son 'utterly ruined' sounds bleak and catastrophic, and the idea that the daughter's husband is 'an hereditary madman' suggests that she becomes the victim of her partner's instability. The exclamation mark emphasizes the alarming nature of the relationship.

3a The writer lists consequences which she connects to the mother's reading of novels. Copy and complete the table below to record these consequences and give each one a danger rating (with 1 being the least dangerous and 5 the most dangerous).

Consequence	Danger rating
Not cleaning the house	1
Children neglected	2
Husband arrested	3
Son quits school and vanishes in Australia	4
Daughter marries a madman	5

3b How has the writer structured her presentation of these consequences? What effect does this create?

Sample answer

The consequences of reading novels are listed in escalating order, building up the picture to one of increasing alarm. This increases the tension and drama of the text, gripping the reader who wants to read on to find out how bad things can possibly get.

4a Look again at the opening and closing paragraphs of the extract. Explain any connections you can find between these.

Sample answer

Both the opening and closing paragraphs focus on the mother. The closing paragraph takes us further back in time to when the woman first married, when she was 'a lovely, clever girl', before she devoted 'herself to novel reading'. The idea that novel reading is 'wicked' in the opening paragraph is echoed in the final paragraph with the reference to 'intoxication' which implies that something else has taken over control of a life, something devilish and powerful.

4b How effective do you think the closing paragraph is? Give reasons for your answer.

Sample answer

I think that the closing paragraph is effective in completing the picture of utter devastation of a family, however, it is so extreme that one can't help question its accuracy. Maybe the daughter did marry someone with less money than her father, but perhaps he was a good man and his mental health issues could be resolved or managed in a way that enabled them to live happy lives. The comparison with intoxication is also questionable. Many forms of intoxication are temporary and can be recovered from. I think that most people seek some escapism from time to time, and in comparison to other options, reading novels seems relatively harmless. The writer of this extract is perhaps rather alarmist and overreacting. I don't think many people would see reading novels as dangerous nowadays.

2.3 'Would you like to sit on the floor?' by Roger Callan, 1999

Basic reading skills

1 **The writer of this article compares the classroom in the school William Shakespeare attended 400 years ago with a modern-day classroom.**

a List three things that the writer says are similar.

Wooden desks; desks positioned in rows; teacher's desk at the front

b List three things that the writer says are different.

Caning is forbidden; science labs; computers

2 **What are the three main types of learner the writer identifies in the article?**

Global, analytic, integrated

3 **Look at the following learning techniques and decide whether they are most appropriate for an auditory, visual, tactile or kinesthetic learner.**

Reading a textbook - visual

Conducting an experiment - tactile

Going to a museum - kinesthetic

Listening to a lecture - auditory

4 **According to the writer, what type of school finds it easiest to adapt their classroom to accommodate students' different learning styles? Explain why this is.**

Primary school classrooms are easiest to adapt to different learning styles because there is more choice about seating, different areas of the classroom and provision of personal stereos.

5 **Using your own words, explain what happened when a school in South Carolina identified the individual learning styles of its students.**

The school results increased so dramatically that officials had to go and check that students weren't cheating.

6 **Look again at the final paragraph.**

a Quote the mantra that the writer includes here.

'Teacher, if I don't learn the way you teach, why don't you teach the way I learn?'

b Why do you think the writer refers to this as a mantra? Explain your ideas.

> **Sample answer**
>
> I think the writer refers to this as a mantra because he believes that if it is repeated often enough it will help to embed the meaning and awareness into the minds of the reader (and people who run schools). A mantra is traditionally a chant used to help meditation.

Advanced reading skills

1 **The lead paragraph of a newspaper article should give the reader information on what the article is about.**

a Look again at the lead paragraph. Using your own words, summarize what the article is about.

This article is about how the place where you learn and the style in which you learn can make a big difference to your results.

b Do you think this is an effective opening paragraph? Give reasons for your answer.

> **Sample answer**
>
> This is an effective opening paragraph because most people are very interested in how to get the best exam results, for themselves, for their children, or for their students. Good exam results can open up a lot of opportunities in terms of training, jobs and higher education.

2a **Pick out evidence from the text that supports the view that students learn in different ways.**

It is backed up by 30 years of research, based on a project run by St John's University in New York City.

2b **How does the writer make this evidence sound authoritative? You could comment on the following phrases:**

- **'based on more than 30 years of research'**
- **'104-question learning style inventory'**
- **'devised by academics'**

> **Sample answer**
>
> The evidence sounds authoritative because of the length of time that has been invested in the project, 'thirty years of research', and the thorough evaluation of a student's preferences, using a '104-question learning style inventory'. Because the inventory is 'devised by academics', the implication is that these people must know what they are doing because they are pioneers in the field and have researched it thoroughly.

3a **Find three quotations which suggest the negative effects of failing to accommodate different learning styles.**

'school frequently offers only discomfort, misunderstanding and even failure'; 'school can be a source of boredom and misery'; 'some students' grades declined'

3b Choose one of your selected quotations and explain how it uses language to suggest these negative effects.

Sample answer

The first quotation uses a pattern of three (tricolon) to emphasize the negative effects. Its use of the word 'only' shows how limiting the outcome is. The word 'even' signifies the worst possible scenario, which adds weight to the point being made.

4 This article was included in the education section of *The Independent* newspaper. What changes would you make to the article to make it more interesting to a general reader?

Sample answer

To make this article more appealing to the general reader, it could use a direct address, including the terms 'you' and 'your'. It might also include some rhetorical questions and exclamations to retain the reader's attention. Shorter sentences and a summary of the research findings might mean general readers keep their focus on the article and don't get bored with the details. A slightly different layout might make the article more accessible, for example, the use of bullet points listing different types of learners and learning styles. Also, references to extremely successful people who might not have achieved academically would draw the readers' attention, and also appear to add weight to the argument for a more flexible approach to learning in schools.

3.1 'Roald Dahl and me' by David Walliams, 2009

Basic reading skills

1 **Create a list of five factual statements based on information from the text. The first one has been done for you.**

Before he wrote his first novel, Walliams re-read some children's books.

Roald Dahl is one of the most popular children's authors.

Roald Dahl appeared regularly on television in the 1970s and 1980s.

Roald Dahl wrote *The Twits, Danny the Champion of the Word, The BFG, George's Marvellous Medicine, The Witches* and *Fantastic Mr Fox*, among others.

Roald Dahl was 6ft 6in tall.

2 **Look at the last two sentences in the first paragraph. David Walliams writes: 'This last one instantly made me want to give up writing. It was perfect.' Explain in your own words what he is implying.**

Sample answer

He is implying that he felt *Charlie and the Chocolate Factory* was so faultless and wonderful that he himself could never write anything as good as this, so he felt put off from even starting to write his own novel.

3 **Look again at the second paragraph. Identify the two Roald Dahl books that David Walliams contrasts and explain the key difference between these books.**

The two Roald Dahl books that David Walliams contrasts are *Danny the Champion of the World* and the *BFG*. He points out that the former could happen in the real world, but the *BFG* could not. It is too fantastical.

4 **David Walliams writes that 'Dahl is the master of cruelty'. List three examples that Walliams gives of how Dahl is cruel in his fiction.**

Mike Teavee is shrunk. Augustus Gloop falls into the chocolate river and is dragged away through a pipe. George kills his grandmother.

5 **Look at the fifth paragraph. David Walliams describes seeing Roald Dahl on television.**

a Explain what he means when he says, 'he was not a great ambassador for his work'.

Roald Dahl did not come across as a particularly attractive celebrity when promoting his work because he was odd-looking, a bit scary, rather weird and cross in his manner, and slightly cold towards the children he spoke to.

b Choose two words of your own to describe his impression of the writer.

Sample answer

Distant, unattractive

6 **In the final paragraph of his article, David Walliams writes that readers enjoy the 'pure pleasure of luxuriating in Dahl's imagination'. In your own words, describe what he means.**

Sample answer

He means that readers enjoy living in the imaginative world that Dahl created in his stories.

Advanced reading skills

1 **It is clear that David Walliams admires Roald Dahl's work.**

a Write down three features that he especially likes.

His genius with names; the lack of rules and morality; the variety in his stories.

b If you had to give one overall reason for David Walliams' admiration, which would it be? How can you tell?

Sample answer

I think the lack of rules and morality attract David Walliams to Roald Dahl's work the most. He likes the fact that things don't always end in a predictable way and that the endings aren't always neatly tied up and balanced. They are 'anarchic'.

2 **Look at the opening sentence of the article. David Walliams writes: 'Before I started writing my first children's novel, I made a big mistake'.**
Instead of the adjective 'big', he could have chosen major, large, significant or enormous.

However, he chooses to use a short, simple word.

a If you were choosing a word instead of 'big', which of those four would you use? Explain why.

Sample answer

I would use the word 'enormous' because it is a fun word that is often used to exaggerate something, and conveys the feeling of something beyond the normal.

b Explain why you think David Walliams chose to use the short, simple word 'big'.

Sample answer

I think he uses the word 'big' because the phrase 'big mistake' is often used in a comical way. It is also a very simple word so everyone knows what it means and is curious about what this mistake could be.

3 **In the third paragraph, David Walliams writes about Roald Dahl's characters, especially the children at the heart of his books. He writes: 'He never gives them magical powers or makes them secret agents.'**

He presents this as a positive feature of Roald Dahl's stories. Explain what you think he means and why you agree or disagree with his opinion.

Sample answer

I think Walliams is making the point that by making the children fairly ordinary, Dahl's readers can identify with them readily and imagine themselves as that particular character, facing the same situation and finding similar solutions.

4 **Look at these other features that David Walliams identifies in Roald Dahl's writing:**

- **'Lack of conventional morality'**
- **'Master of cruelty'**
- **'Anarchic'**

Explain how David Walliams gives you the impression that these are positive features.

David Walliams presents these as positive features because of the effect they have on children as they read: the 'cruelty' and the 'lack of conventional morality' excites children, who find them 'compelling', which means they want to read on. Children enjoy feeling that they are entering 'a thrillingly dangerous world' in Dahl's novels. The 'anarchic' nature of the stories appeals to children because they are unpredictable and rarely have 'everything in their rightful place'. They are often illogical, 'like a dream narrative'.

5 **Which point in the article do you most agree with or disagree with? Write a few sentences to explain your viewpoint. Quote David Walliams' words if it helps you to support your case.**

Sample answer

Walliams says that 'children are the toughest audience'. I agree with this statement because children tend to speak their minds and don't pretend to enjoy something if they really don't. They often cannot disguise their reactions to things in the same way that adults might, so there is no 'censorship' of their feelings and opinions. This can be refreshing but it can also be daunting if they are judging your work. They may seem unkind, but they are usually just being honest.

3.2 'A passion for books' by Sue Townsend, 1992

Basic reading skills

1 **Re-read the first paragraph.**

a List three facts the writer gives in this paragraph.

She couldn't read until she was eight; her teacher was a woman; she was 46 when she wrote this text.

b List two opinions the writer gives in this paragraph.

Her teacher was nasty; she looked like an irritated badger.

2 **Now look at the second paragraph. Using your own words, summarize how the writer learned to read.**

Sample answer

When the writer was ill her mother bought her some 'William' books. At first, she just enjoyed the illustrations, but then tried to make out the captions and with her mother's help learned to read words and full sentences.

3 **'There should have been a hundred-gun salute. The Red Arrows should have flown overhead. The night sky should have blazed with fireworks.' What impression does this quotation give you of the writer's emotions when she learned to read?**

Sample answer

She felt that it was a really important, momentous occasion, worthy of great celebration.

4 **Pick out three quotations that suggest the writer was a keen reader when she was young.**

'I was addicted to print'; 'I would often read three books a day'; 'reading became the most important thing in my life'

5 **What suggests the librarian didn't believe the writer had read all the books that she borrowed from the library?**

The librarian asked the writer questions about the books because she suspected that she hadn't really read them properly and was just 'showing off', boasting that she had.

6 **How does the writer suggest that reading was a 'secret obsession'? Using information from the text, explain why you think the writer had to keep her reading a secret.**

Sample answer

The writer says that she would pretend not to read if anyone came into a room. I think she kept her reading a secret because it was an unusual hobby among her family and friends. The adults in her life thought that her reading was a 'sign of derangement', meaning that they thought she was very odd. Some people warned her that so much reading was dangerous, making her reluctant to read in public.

Advanced reading skills

1 **Look at the first paragraph and identify the simile the writer uses to describe her teacher. Explain the effect this creates.**

The simile 'looked like a dyspeptic badger' makes the writer's teacher sound like a bad-tempered, rather inelegant animal, that shuffles along with its long snout near the ground, never looking up or out, as if she was always preoccupied and rather antisocial.

2 **Pick out all the different places the writer says she used to read.**

a What impression does this give you of the writer?

The writer mentions that she read in bed, at breakfast, on the way to school, during school breaks, in the cloakroom and on bus journeys. This creates the impression of a rather solitary child, who prefers to engage with characters in her books rather than with real people around her.

b Explain the effect this use of repetition creates.

The repetition of 'I read' and 'reading' reinforces how obsessive the writer was about her books. They accompanied her everywhere, and she took every opportunity to delve into them.

3 **The writer says: 'When reading I half expected my head to explode and hit the ceiling. It didn't put me off.'**

a Explain how the writer uses humour in this quotation.

The image of the writer's head exploding is comical because it is so absurd. Knowledge isn't anything physical, so ideas and stories don't really take up any space in your brain.

b Pick out another quotation that you think creates humour and explain your choice.

Sample answer

I think the author's reference to great celebrations such as 'a hundred-gun salute' and 'fireworks' creates humour because the image they create of a huge national celebration is a comic contrast to the very personal, fairly modest achievement of someone learning to read.

4 **Which book do you think was the most important to the writer in her childhood? Refer to evidence from the text to support your choice.**

Sample answer

I think that *Jane Eyre* was the most important book to the writer in her childhood because it was the 'first book' that she ever 'lost a night's sleep over'. She goes on to explain how she could not put the book down, reading in bed, reading while eating breakfast, and reading at every opportunity in school.

5 **'Reading became the most important thing in my life.' Explain how the writer uses language to suggest how important reading was to her.**

Sample answer

The writer uses words like 'passion' and 'obsession' to describe how she felt about reading, emphasizing how it took over her life and eclipsed everything else going on around her. Her description of how she was prepared to endure physical discomfort in order to keep reading shows her level of commitment, for example, she read in bed even though her 'fingers and arms froze', her 'nails went blue', and she read until dawn, despite her eyes drooping, but she 'had to read on'.

6 **Look at the following student's statement about the text:**

I think books were the writer's friend.

Argue for or against this statement, drawing on evidence from the text.

Sample answer

In some ways books were the writer's friend because she was far more interested in what happened to the characters in them than the other people around her. She was always eager to spend time in their company, to find out more about them and their circumstances. She says she 'loved Jane' and had to keep reading to find out 'who had started the fire' and who the 'mad creature in the attic' was. However, she also admits that she 'felt very lonely'. This highlights the fact that books aren't real friends – you can't discuss things with books or exchange ideas. Reading is a one-way friendship in some ways.

3.3 'Juvenilia' by Arthur Conan Doyle, 1893

Basic reading skills

1 **Look again at the first paragraph. Using your own words, briefly summarize what happened in the first story Sir Arthur Conan Doyle wrote.**

A tiger ate a man.

2 **Where does he say his first story is now?**

In an old family bureau

3 **Look at the second paragraph beginning, 'Then came my second book...'. Pick out the quotation that you think best suggests that the writer was a keen reader as a child.**

'four years had elapsed, which were mainly spent in reading'

4 **List five exciting situations that the writer claims to have experienced through his reading.**

Sailing in the Pacific; sitting on a charging buffalo; setting the prairie on fire; being chased by bloodhounds; shooting down rapids.

5 **What payment does he receive from his classmates for his storytelling at public school?**

Pastry tarts

Advanced reading skills

1 **Re-read the opening paragraph. What impression do you get of Sir Arthur Conan Doyle as a six-year-old?**

Sample answer

I get the impression that when he was six, Doyle was an imaginative, creative boy who was enthusiastic and meticulous when starting a project but didn't always think it through to its logical conclusion. The evidence for this is that he created a picture book about a man getting eaten by a tiger, but then didn't know how to finish his story. He obviously liked thinking about dramatic and gory detail as he says he 'described at some length, both verbally and pictorially the untimely end' of his character.

2 **Look again at the paragraph beginning, 'I do not think that life has any joy…'. How does the language used help to create a sense of the excitement the writer found in the stories he read?**

Sample answer

Doyle creates a sense of excitement when recounting his early reading adventures by using the first person with active verbs, such as 'I had traversed every sea', 'I had creased horses', 'I had shot down rapids'. He describes very physical outdoor adventures, often including danger and violence, for example, he mentions torture, harpooning, shooting, running, being under water and clinging 'on to the leg of an albatross'. The sentences tend to be multi-clause as he describes different episodes of his adventures with each activity in a separate clause, but linked as a sequence of energetic, breathless events, echoing an adrenaline-fuelled race to escape and survive.

3 **Read the following quotation from the extract: 'It was all more real than the reality.'**

Explain whether you think this extract supports or contradicts this statement about the power of stories. Give reasons for your answer, referring to the text of the extract.

Sample answer

I think this extract supports the statement because many things in life turn out to be less exciting than you expect, but in your imagination, excitement levels can be exactly what you want them to be; you create your own reality in your mind. Some of the descriptions in the extract seem unrealistic and unlikely to happen in real life, for example, falling into the ocean and surviving by clinging on to the leg of an albatross. However, in the world of imagination, all things are possible, and the imagination is just another type of reality with even greater scope than the actual world.

4 **The writer describes his real experience of shooting bears and harpooning whales as 'flat'. How might we describe these activities nowadays, and why?**

Sample answer

Today, many people feel that the hunting of wild animals for sport is morally wrong, particularly as overhunting means that many species are endangered, and that killing for pleasure is cruel and unnecessary. Hunting for food in order to survive is generally recognized as necessary in the animal world, but humans have more control over their environment and can make choices not to hunt or even eat animals. Nowadays there is greater sensitivity about the welfare of animals and the extent to which they suffer when being hunted.

5 **How does the writer create a sense of his growing power as a storyteller? Think about how both language and structure are used to build a picture of him as an author and convey his abilities as a storyteller.**

Sample answer

This extract is structured to follow the chronology of Doyle's development as a storyteller. It begins with his childhood attempts to create a simple picture book, follows his increasing escapism into reading through his childhood, then the development of his oral storytelling to his classmates ('elevated on to a desk') through which he learned how to grab and retain the audience's attention, getting them caught up in his imaginative tales ('in my power'), thereby preparing the way to hone his ideas and craft for writing his second book. He mentions that he was 'born to be a member of the Authors' Society', meaning that he learned that his storytelling skills were valuable at an early age and he learned how to extract some profit from them.

4.1 'Hotel unveils ROBOT butler' by Josh Gardner, 2014

Basic reading skills

1a What is the name of the robot butler, mentioned in the first paragraph?

A.L.O. is the robot butler's name.

1b Explain why you think this is an appropriate name.

This is an appropriate name because it sounds like the greeting 'hello', which suggests that the robot is friendly and willing to help.

2a In the second paragraph, what is the term 'robot butler' shortened to?

Botlr is the shortened form of 'robot butler'.

2b Again, explain why you think this is an appropriate name.

This is a clever name because it combines the 'bot' from 'robot' with the letters 'lr' which together make the word sound like 'butler' which is the robot's function.

3a Identify three fictional robots that the robot butler is compared to.

Wall-E, R2D2, Rosie

3b Choose one of these fictional robots and explain why this comparison is appropriate.

Sample answer

Wall-E is an appropriate comparison because Wall-E is a character in a film that is left on earth by humans to tidy up the garbage. He carries out his duties for hundreds of years, in a diligent, dedicated way. Botlr also has a servant-like role, ready to do the bidding of humans.

4 How does the robot butler respond if it receives a positive review? Pick the correct statement from the list below.

It does a happy dance.

5 The article says: 'Starwood and Savioke hope to use the robot as a way to funnel existing human staff towards more sensitive tasks rather than a death knell for bellhops'. Using your own words, explain what the term 'death knell' means here.

'Death knell' literally means the bell that rings to signify a funeral – the end of a life. It is used here to refer to the end of the job of bellhops.

Advanced reading skills

1 Explain how this article gives you the impression that the robot butler is a worthwhile invention.

The article suggests that the robot butler is a worthwhile invention because it says that human staff can be used for more sensitive tasks, rather than fetching and carrying for hotel guests. It also describes the robot as an 'accomplished drone', moving 'at a fast clip of up to 4mph' and mentions the 'look of delight on those guests who receive a room delivery from a robot'.

2 The writer uses lots of short, single-sentence paragraphs. Pick out some examples and explain why you think the writer has chosen to structure the article in this way.

The writer uses single-sentence paragraphs to deliver bite-sized information in an accessible, speedy style, so that the reader can skim through the text quickly, picking out key bits of information. For example 'The 3-foot tall robot... name tag' gives a complete description of the robot's appearance very succinctly. The sentence 'So how exactly will guests experience A.L.O?' acts like a subheading, with the explanation below. This helps the reader to navigate the structure of the text easily and swiftly.

3 The article includes direct speech from Brian McGuinness and Steve Cousins. Why do you think the writer has chosen to do this? Explain the effect created by the use of direct speech from each person quoted in the text.

The direct speech from Brian McGuinness explains why A.L.O. was chosen by the Starwood company, and gives a human touch to the business deal. His reference to R2D2 being 'my favourite childhood robot' adds some humour and a personal touch, and is a sentiment that many readers can probably relate to.

The direct speech from Steve Cousins states that the people who created A.L.O. enjoy the reception of their robot from the hotel guests. Cousins is the CEO of the company that created A.L.O. which means that he was in charge of the people who developed the robot, so he can give an 'insider's' perspective.

4 **Do you think this article would have appeared in the technology section or the travel section of *The Daily Mail*? Refer to evidence from the text to support your answer.**

Sample answer

I think this article is more likely to feature in the travel section of a newspaper because the focus is on the experience of using a robot in a hotel rather than the technical details of how it has been developed, what stages it went through, what components it uses or comparative developments.

4.2 'The servantless house', 1921

Basic reading skills

1 **Look again at the paragraph beginning 'The general idea…'.**

a What does the writer suggest this article is going to be about?

The writer suggests this article is going to be about the cost of labour-saving machinery in ordinary houses.

b What reason does the writer give for writing this article?

The reason for the article is to investigate whether labour-saving machinery is really too expensive.

2 **Identify the two types of people who don't employ servants, according to the writer.**

People who can't afford servants and people who prefer not to.

3 **Look again at the paragraph beginning 'In pre-war days…'.**

a List three tasks the writer suggests that servants carried out in this period.

Polishing brass; cleaning stair-rods; sweeping carpets

b List three reasons the writer gives why servants might not be able to carry out these tasks.

Servants may be unaffordable, unobtainable or undesirable.

4 **Look at the section entitled 'Relative costs'.**

a How much in total does the writer say a homeowner would spend on a maid in a year?

£98

b How much in total does the writer say a homeowner would spend buying essential labour-saving devices?

£60

c Re-read the paragraph beginning, 'The fact that this is…'. Explain another advantage of buying essential labour-saving devices that the writer gives here.

Labour-saving devices, once purchased, will last for years, whereas a servant needs to be paid every year.

5 **Does the writer recommend employing a maid or buying labour-saving devices?**

Buying labour-saving devices

Advanced reading skills

1 **In this article, the writer compares the cost of purchasing such devices with the cost of employing a servant to carry out these jobs for you. Do you think the writer presents this comparison in an unbiased way? Refer to evidence from the text to support your answer.**

Sample answer

I think the writer is biased in favour of buying gadgets over employing a servant because he or she does not consider the advantages of employing a servant, such as providing employment, offering some company for the housewife, and the flexibility of having a servant to do work that is unexpected. Also, the writer doesn't consider that some labour-saving devices will break down and need repairing, and they don't last indefinitely so will ultimately need replacing.

2 **The writer uses the rule of three to emphasize certain points. Look at this example: 'Mechanical labour is more certain, less tiring and altogether more reliable than human labour.'**

a How does this use of the rule of three support the writer's viewpoint?

This rule of three states three advantages of using 'mechanical labour', emphasizing the advantages to the reader in a short, precise statement.

b Pick out another quotation from the article that uses the rule of three and explain the effect this creates.

The writer also uses the rule of three to emphasize the additional costs of keeping a servant: 'the cost in wear and tear, in breakages, and in lack of economy of fuel and light'. This creates the effect of stacking up the disadvantages into a strong argument for not employing a servant.

3 **How does the structure of the article help the reader to evaluate which is the best option: employing a maid or buying labour-saving devices?**

Sample answer

The structure of the article is carefully planned so that it follows a logical sequence in order to convince the reader of the value of its argument in favour of labour-saving devices. The opening paragraph states clearly what many people believe – that labour-saving machinery is too expensive for ordinary homes. The next paragraph outlines the problem faced by housewives – how to get their work done. The third paragraph looks at why this wasn't a problem for pre-war households, but explains why it has become a problem because of the shortage and expense of servants.

The subheading 'Relative costs' sets out a clear comparison of the expense associated with a maid and that of labour-saving devices. The two lists look very clear and accessible, and their use is effective in weighing up the argument with the use of figures, which readers associate with facts that cannot be disputed. It makes the evaluation seem decisive and indisputable.

The penultimate paragraph adds a further argument in favour of buying labour-saving devices, ending with the description of them as 'a thoroughly good investment'. The final paragraph refers back to the housewife running the house more effectively without a servant and implies that she will in fact have more time and freedom 'for other interests'.

4 **This newspaper article was first published in 1921. Explain how the language and ideas in the article reflect the time in which it was written.**

Sample answer

The ideas in this article reflect a dilemma and difficulties that very few people face nowadays; today only the rich have servants and most 'ordinary' homes have no need for them. However, it was obviously a choice that people in the 1920s had to consider and were concerned about.

The mention of certain household tasks reflects the time in which it was written, for example, not many households nowadays have 'brass' to polish, or 'stair-rods' to clean, and most people have vacuum cleaners rather 'sweep' their carpets. The salaries and costs that are mentioned seem extremely modest today, but that is because of inflation and a change in currency since this article was written.

The terms 'labour-saving devices' and 'mechanical labour' also reflect the historical period, as nowadays we would refer to 'household or domestic gadgets' that help us to maintain our homes.

Another feature that reflects the time in which the article was written is the emphasis of housework being the responsibility of a woman. Today, most households believe that domestic work should be shared between everyone living in a household, whatever their gender and age. Although this work sometimes falls more heavily on some members than others, there is an increasing recognition that it shouldn't just be a woman's responsibility, particularly as so many women also work outside the home nowadays.

4.3 'Duties of the Lady's Maid' from *Mrs Beeton's Book of Household Management* by Isabella Beeton, 1861

Basic reading skills

1 **Re-read the first paragraph.**

a List three things which a lady's maid should do to get the dressing-room ready.

Sweep the carpet; clean the mirror; polish the furniture.

b Pick out two quotations that suggest that a lady's maid should take great care when cleaning the room.

'sweep them carefully'; 'taking care to penetrate to every corner'

c Look again at the phrase, 'the dressing-room is ready for the mistress when she thinks proper to appear'. Using your own words, explain what you think the writer means here.

Sample answer

I think the writer means that the mistress may still be in bed while all this work is taking place. Or perhaps it refers to when the mistress returns to the dressing-room in the evening in order to 'dress for dinner'.

2 **Which room should the lady's maid prepare after getting the dressing-room ready?**

The bedroom

3 **What does the writer suggest will be one of the main tasks of a lady's maid? Pick out the quotation that suggests this.**

'Plain work' which means everyday sewing and repairs, as opposed to 'fancy work' which is decorative sewing, such as embroidery.

4 **Re-read the paragraph beginning, 'A waiting-maid, who wishes to make herself useful...'. Using your own words, summarize the key advice given here in a single sentence.**

Sample answer

A good maid will help her mistress to dress fashionably and also recycle old clothes into something useful for children.

Advanced reading skills

1 **What impression do you get of the duties of a lady's maid from this extract? Use a spider diagram to collect all the information you can about these from the text.**

Sample answer

Answers might include the following: hard physical work, rather boring, dirty, detailed, repetitive

2 **Which of the following characteristics do you think the extract suggests a lady's maid needs to have? For each one that you select, pick out a quotation from the extract that you think demonstrates the need for this characteristic. The first one has been done for you.**

strong – 'moving every article of furniture that is portable'

diligent – 'taking care to penetrate to every corner'

creative – 'making up dresses which have served one purpose, to serve another also'

dedicated – 'render herself invaluable to her mistress'

thoughtful – 'will study the fashion books with attention'

3 **Read what this student says about the tone of this extract.**

I think the writer creates quite a strict tone – it sounds as if she's ordering you about.

Do you agree or disagree with this statement? Justify your answer with reference to the text.

Sample answer

I agree with this statement because the text is written a bit like an instruction manual, using modal verbs such as 'should' and 'will'. The advice is given in quite a formal, no-nonsense manner because this book isn't written for entertainment, but to give guidance about duties and responsibilities. There is an impersonal tone throughout, referring to the maid as 'she' rather than the more informal 'you'.

4 **Write down three details from the text that show it was written in the 19th century.**

'having previously strewed the room with moist tea-leaves'; 'emptied all slops'; 'The lady's-maid may thus render herself invaluable to her mistress, and increase her own happiness in so doing.'

5.1 'Top tips for creative writing' by Jacqueline Wilson, 2016

Basic reading skills

1 **In her first tip, Jacqueline Wilson gives three ways that she gets ideas. Which of these is not one that she mentions?**

B. Overhearing the conversations of a stranger.

2 **Of the sources of ideas that Jacqueline Wilson mentions, which occurs the least frequently? How can you tell this?**

Ideas from other people – she uses the word 'occasionally'.

3 **From reading the whole blog, decide which of these statements are true and which are false. Be ready to discuss and justify your decision on each statement.**

A. The most frequent question is what do your characters look like. False
B. Everyone gets their ideas in different ways. True
C. Recording ideas on paper will help you later. True
D. Staring at a blank screen helps with the writing process. False
E. Writing very quickly can sometimes be a helpful technique. True
F. Editors are like teachers, but more demanding. True
G. Once you have lots of good ideas on paper, rewriting isn't usually necessary. False

Advanced reading skills

1 **Look again at the section 'How to Create Characters'. Here, Jacqueline Wilson writes: 'Did you ever have imaginary friends when you were little?'**

In your own words, explain how this use of a question to the reader helps her to communicate her advice in this section.

Sample answer

By asking this question, Jacqueline Wilson is trying to remind her readers of something that they may have been familiar with when they were little children. This will help them to understand how she imagines her characters now by comparing it with those childlike games.

2 **In some parts of her blog, Jacqueline Wilson uses exclamation marks at the end of sentences, for example: 'This is the difficult bit!'**

Explain what effect the use of an exclamation mark has here.

The exclamation mark draws attention to the statement. It emphasizes that starting a story is not easy.

3 **Jacqueline Wilson clearly wants to end her stories in an interesting way. In your own words, explain what she tries to do with the endings of her stories.**

Sample answer

She tries to make her stories end in a way that will satisfy her readers, so she tries to take her time in writing the ending and think things through very carefully. It doesn't necessarily have to be an explicit ending though. Sometimes she leaves the ending open to the reader's interpretation.

4 **Look at how Jacqueline Wilson uses language in her blog. Focus on this sentence:**

A. So, let's say you've taken your time over your ending and are pleased with your story.

She could instead have written it like this to communicate the same meaning:

B. Let us assume that you have deliberated over your ending and are satisfied with your story.

What differences do you notice between versions A and B? Use these prompts for a detailed response to the writer's language choices:

- **Version A starts with the word 'So'. The effect of this is...**
- **Version A uses contracted forms of words ('let's' and 'you've' rather than 'let us' and 'you have'). The effect of this is...**
- **Version A uses 'say' rather than 'assume' and 'taken your time' rather than 'deliberated'. The effect of this is...**
- **Overall, I prefer version A/B because...**

Sample answer

Jacqueline Wilson uses an informal chatty style of language in her blog, so that her readers feel comfortable with her and regard her almost as a friend, rather than someone who is simply telling them what to do. In the example sentence, Wilson starts with the colloquial use of 'So' which sets the conversational tone, then goes on to use the contractions, 'let's' and 'you've', which continue the informal style. Her choice of phrasing, such as 'taken your time', has an everyday tone which feels intimate and friendly rather than judgemental and dictatorial. I prefer Version A because it is accessible and conveys goodwill and encouragement. Version B is much more formal and impersonal.

5.2 Letter to Joan Lancaster by C. S. Lewis, 1956

Basic reading skills

1 **Re-read the opening paragraph of the letter.**

a What four things does C. S. Lewis say Joan has described very well?

The place, the people, the night, the feeling of it all.

b What does C. S. Lewis say Joan hasn't described?

The thing itself

c Which other writer does the same thing according to C. S. Lewis?

Wordsworth

2 **Based on the text, decide whether the following statements are true or false.**

- **Only people in Southern England speak 'Good English'.** False
- **There is no such thing as 'Good English'.** False
- **'Good English' changes over time.** True
- **'Good English' is the language spoken by educated people.** True

3 **Why does C. S. Lewis recommend using the word 'keep' instead of 'implement'?**

It is better to use a plain, direct word than a long, vague one.

4 **Find a phrase or sentence in the text that suggests C. S. Lewis likes writing that appeals to his readers' emotions.**

'describe it so that we'll be terrified'

5 **Look at the sentence: 'Don't use words too big for the subject.' Decide which of the following statements match what the writer is suggesting.**

Use words as precisely as you can.

Sometimes it is worth using simpler words so that the more complex ones will have a real impact when you use them.

Advanced reading skills

1 **Look again at the sentence: 'If you become a writer you'll be trying to describe the *thing* all your life: and lucky if, out of dozens of books, one or two sentences, just for a moment, come near to getting it across.'**

a What might 'the thing' C. S. Lewis writes about be in this instance?

He might mean something meaningful about life, an observation or depiction of something that is a universal truth.

b What does this sentence suggest about the challenges of being a writer?

This sentence suggests that it is very difficult to produce a work that is really significant and powerful.

2 **Which of the following words do you think best describes the tone of C. S. Lewis' letter? Justify your choice with reference to the text.**

Sample answer

I think that 'generous' best describes the tone of this letter, because he is giving away precious knowledge that he has gained over many years of honing his craft as a writer.

3a **C. S. Lewis uses different types of punctuation in the letter. Find examples of the following and for each one, explain the effect the punctuation creates:**

- **dash** – Lewis uses two dashes for parenthesis in the third sentence. He uses it to insert a pause before referring to 'the thing itself' and another pause before continuing with the main sentence.
- **exclamation mark** – Lewis uses an exclamation mark after the words 'And no wonder' in order to

draw attention to the comment. It expresses more of an emotional reaction than just a full stop.

- **colon** – Lewis uses a colon in order to introduce five pieces of advice. This indicates that what follows is in relation to the preceding statement, that is, 'What really matters'.
- **quotation marks** – Lewis uses quotation marks to indicate specific words that he is using as examples during his explanations and in giving advice. The quotation marks help to make the words stand out so the reader can easily see what Lewis is referring to.

3b C. S. Lewis also uses italics in places. Explain why you think he does this. Remember to give examples from the text to support your explanation.

Sample answer

Lewis uses italics to draw attention to certain words, for example, he uses italics when he refers to the 'thing' to emphasize its importance. He also uses italics to refer to specific words, such as the contractions 'amn't I' and 'aren't I'. Lewis also uses italics for the title of the poem the 'Prelude' by Wordsworth. This highlights the fact that it is the name of a written work.

4 Explore which pieces of advice in the letter you find most helpful and explain why they might help you with your own writing.

Sample answer

I find the most useful piece of advice is about not telling the reader how to react to something that is described, but letting the description itself evoke the feeling in the reader. It is very easy to overuse words like 'terrible' and 'delightful' but more challenging to create those feelings through other words. The alternative expressions are likely to be more original and powerful.

I also think that the advice about clarity is important because it's easy to write imprecisely which then leads to the reader getting the wrong impression and not really sharing the writer's vision.

5.3 *The Life of Charlotte Brontë* by Elizabeth Gaskell, 1857

Basic reading skills

1 Why did Charlotte Brontë and her sisters keep their writing a secret from their father?

They didn't want to burden him with the possibility of disappointment on their behalf.

2 Pick out a quotation that suggests that Charlotte Brontë's father had been interested in writing stories when he was younger.

'his own tendency had been towards literature in the days when he was young and hopeful'

3a What did the postman ask Mr Brontë?

The postman asked where Currer Bell was living.

3b What did Mr Brontë reply?

He replied that there was no one by that name living in the parish.

4 Why did Charlotte Brontë finally decide to tell her father that she had published a novel?

Charlotte's sisters persuaded her to tell their father of her writing once *Jane Eyre* was successful.

5 Look again at the dialogue between Charlotte and her father which begins, "Papa, I've been writing a book." Using your own words, summarize Mr Brontë's response to the news Charlotte gives him.

Sample answer

Mr Brontë initially doubts that he'll be able to read his daughter's handwriting, then thinks she must have spent a lot of money getting it printed, and finally is surprised at how good the book is.

6 Look again at the final sentence: 'No one they knew had genius enough to be the author'. What does this suggest about people's opinions of *Jane Eyre?*

This suggests that people thought *Jane Eyre* must be written by a genius because it was exceptionally good.

Advanced reading skills

1 ***The Life of Charlotte Brontë*** **was first published in 1857. Pick out one example of dialogue that you think best indicates the time this book was written. Explain your choice.**

Sample answer

'it is much better than likely' – This statement uses phrasing that would be rare nowadays. Today we would be more likely to say, 'It is much better than you would think'.

2 **The author writes of Mr Brontë, 'his daughters knew how he would have borne ill-success worse for them than for himself'. Explain what you think this means in your own words.**

Sample answer

I think this means that Mr Brontë found it harder to suffer disappointment on behalf of his daughters than for himself.

3 **Which of the following words would you use to describe Mr Brontë's character? Justify your choices with reference to the text.**

Sample answer

I would describe Mr Brontë as 'cautious' and 'anxious' because he is obviously worried about money (the expense of Charlotte getting her book printed) and is extremely sensitive to his daughters' hopes and feelings. He cannot believe that anyone would buy Charlotte's book because no one knows of her, and he feels it extremely unlikely that the book will be good.

4 **What impression do you get of Charlotte Brontë from this extract?**

Sample answer

I get the impression that Charlotte Brontë is a quiet, unassuming person, not wanting to flaunt her success and preferring to remain anonymous. She doesn't tell her father about her writing initially because she doesn't want him to be disappointed on her behalf – this shows great sensitivity and kindness. Her conversation with her father is patient and gentle, breaking the news to him slowly and reassuring him about his eyes, the expense and the reception of her book (via reviews). The fact that the public regard the author of *Jane Eyre* as a 'genius' reinforces the admiration that the writer obviously has for her friend.

6.1 *Travels in West Africa* by Mary Kingsley, 1897

Basic reading skills

1 Look again at the first paragraph. Summarize what the gorillas are doing when Mary Kingsley first spots them.

The gorillas are tearing down fruit and eating it.

2a Now look at the second paragraph. Note down three facts that you learn about the gorillas from this paragraph.

Gorillas can make a whinnying, chattering noise; their arms are very long; they drag their arms with knuckles down.

2b Mary Kingsley says the gorillas 'squattered across the open ground in a most inelegant style'. Using your own words, provide a definition for the word 'squattered'.

Sample answer

Moved around in a position like a squat, with their legs bent and low towards the ground.

3 How can you tell that Mary Kingsley is worried that Wiki will shoot the gorillas?

She puts her hand on his gun.

4 What happens to disturb the gorillas?

Wiki sneezes.

5 Pick one of the following words to describe the gorillas' reaction to the disturbance. Give reasons for your choice.

Sample answer

I think the gorillas were frightened because they left the area very quickly.

Advanced reading skills

1 Write down three words which you think best describe the gorillas that Mary Kingsley observes. Then select a quotation that you think best illustrates each word.

Athletic – 'superbly perfect hand-trapeze performance'

Huge – 'a matter of ten feet at least'

Fast – 'with a celerity that was amazing'

2 Does Mary Kingsley appear to be scared of the gorillas? In a sentence, explain why or why not. Use an example from the text to support your answer.

Sample answer

I don't think Mary Kingsley is scared of the gorillas. She seems to admire them and be fascinated by them. She says 'I watched the gorillas with great interest…'.

3 In order to describe to the reader what her encounter with gorillas was like, Mary Kingsley uses words and phrases relating to different senses. Pick out a quotation to show how she uses each of these senses and explain the effect this creates:

- Sight – 'One of these had clinging to her a young fellow, with beautiful wavy black hair with just a kink in it'. This quotation describes the detail of how the scene looked, focusing in on the quality of the youngster's black hair.
- Sound – 'an explosive sneeze'. This quotation conveys the impression of a very sudden, rather alarming, dramatic noise – the sneeze was startling in that quiet environment, like an explosion.
- Touch – 'gripped'. This verb conveys the idea of someone being assertive and determined. It shows how strongly Wiki did not want Mary to fire the gun.

4 This text was written in the late 19th century. Look at the following sentence and comment on how this suggests when the text was written: 'Heavens! think I, this gentleman's going to have a fit; it's lost we are entirely this time.'

Sample answer

The order of the subject and verb seems old-fashioned nowadays, for example, 'think I' and 'it's lost we are' would be phrased 'I think' and 'we are lost' today. The exclamation 'Heavens' also feels rather dated to a reader today. The use of the semi-colon is less frequent in modern language.

5 **Find an example of humour in the text and explain what it suggests about Kingsley's personality.**

Sample answer

The description of Wiki trying to subdue his urge to sneeze is comical. The exaggerated expressions, noises and movement build up a ridiculous comic picture and show that the writer could see the funny side of human behaviour, even in a potentially dangerous situation.

6.2 'Chimpanzees - Bridging the gap' by Jane Goodall, 1993

Basic reading skills

1 **Re-read the opening paragraph.**

a List two facts about chimpanzee children.

They suckle (drink milk from their mothers) for five years. Older children travel with their mother for three or four years, even after the birth of another child.

b Choose three of the following words to describe the relationship between different members of a chimpanzee family:

loving; long-lasting; supportive

c 'Chimpanzees, like humans, can learn by observation and imitation.' Using your own words, explain what this means.

Sample answer

Chimpanzees watch what others do and copy them.

d What do the Gombe chimpanzees use tools to do?

Use sticks to get ants out of their nests.

e What do the chimpanzees of West Africa use tools to do?

They use a hammer and anvil technique to open the hard outer shell of fruits.

2 **Jane Goodall is a scientist.**

a Pick out three examples of scientific language that you can find in the essay.

'There is proof'; 'language acquisition experiments'; 'evidence for sophisticated mental performances'

b Explain what effect this use of scientific language has on you as a reader.

This scientific language reassures the reader that the writer has studied the chimpanzees in depth and the conclusions are drawn from real evidence, rather than just speculation.

3 **Find an example of chimpanzee behaviour that suggests the 'dark side to their nature'.**

Sample answer

They can be 'brutal' and engage in a form of warfare.

4 **Pick out three more similarities between humans and chimpanzees.**

Many of their gestures are similar to those that humans use, for example, kissing, holding hands, tickling. They can solve problems using reasoning, and they can plan for the short-term future.

5 **What does the writer suggest is responsible for the human race's success as a species?**

The very rapid development of the human brain

Advanced reading skills

1 **Jane Goodall writes that the postures and gestures that chimpanzees use to communicate are 'uncannily' like many of our own. Explain what the word 'uncannily' means here and why you think the writer has chosen to use this word.**

In this context 'uncannily' means surprisingly. I think the writer has chosen to use this word because it conveys the sense of things being difficult to understand and slightly unsettling, as if it disturbs our trust in our traditional perception of things.

2 **Choose one sentence from the essay that you think best sums up the writer's attitude to chimpanzees. Write it down and then explain why you have chosen it.**

Sample answer

'the line dividing "man" from "beast" has become increasingly blurred' – This quotation sums up the core of the writer's observations, that is, that chimpanzees do have human-like qualities and abilities.

3 **Summarize in a paragraph the argument Jane Goodall presents in this essay.**

Sample answer

By detailing the behaviour of chimpanzees, in their families and wider groups, the writer draws attention to the sophistication of the chimps, their abilities, relationships and care for one another. Their similarity to humans means we should take more responsibility for treating them fairly, giving them 'rights' to dignity and freedom - the same right that humans enjoy.

4 **Read one student's comment about the essay.**

I think the writer of this article is biased.

Explain what this student means and whether you agree or disagree with their statement. Refer to the text to support your view.

Sample answer

I don't think the writer of this article is biased because her views seem to be based on thorough research and evidence gained through many years of close observation and study. The chimpanzees have obviously been observed in many different scenarios, and during a variety of experiments, so the conclusions drawn are scientific rather than just opinions.

6.3 'Penguin swims 5,000 miles every year for reunion with the man who saved his life' by Alison Lynch, 2016

Basic reading skills

1 **What is the name of the fisherman who saved the penguin's life?**

Joao Pereira de Souza

2 **How did the fisherman save the penguin?**

He cleaned the oil off the penguin and fed him fish.

3 **What name did the fisherman give to the penguin?**

Dindim

4 **How long did the penguin first stay with the fisherman?**

11 months

5 **The fisherman says, 'I love the penguin like it's my own child and I believe the penguin loves me.' Pick out two quotations from the article that support this statement.**

'He lays on my lap'; 'lets me give him showers'

6 **How does the writer suggest the relationship between the penguin and the man is so unusual?**

She quotes the biologist saying, 'I have never seen anything like this before'.

7 **What impression do you get of the writer's view of this news story? Support your answer with reference to the text.**

Sample answer

The writer really likes this story, particularly as she finishes on the comment 'the world seems a kinder place again'. As a journalist, she probably witnesses a lot of trauma and drama in life, but this story of devotion is touchingly simple and straightforward.

Advanced reading skills

1 **Look at the opening sentence of the article. How does it make the reader want to read on?**

The story is introduced as 'Today's most heartwarming story' which makes the reader keen to read on in order to experience a burst of positivity and happy emotions.

2 **Newspapers and online news sites compete with each other for reader attention and page clicks. Find a piece of evidence from the article that suggests this news story has been covered by other media outlets, for example, newspapers and television channels.**

There is mention of Globo TV and an interview with Joao, plus a reference to *The Independent*.

3 **Read this comment on the text and decide whether you agree or disagree with it: 'This article isn't really news.'**

Give your response to this comment, referring to the text to support your view.

Sample answer

I think this article is news in the sense that it is reporting an event which is unusual and of interest to the general public. It may not be hugely dramatic or significant, but many people will be interested in the level of devotion and affection between the man and the penguin because it is a very rare example of such a relationship. It also makes people question more widely the possible relationships between humans and animals.

4 **The writer has included direct speech from two people in the article.**

a Pick out the two people quoted in the article. Why do you think the writer has chosen to include their voices in this news story?

The writer has chosen to quote Joao because he is giving his own personal recount and opinion of events. It makes the story seem credible and more surprising than an impersonal third-person report. The second quotation is from the biologist who is also a professor. I think the writer includes this to reassure the reader of the validity of the article; an expert confirms that the relationship is very unusual and he has seen it with his own eyes.

b Who else might the writer have chosen to interview and why?

The writer might also have chosen to interview other local fishermen, neighbours or members of Joao's family to corroborate the story.

5 **Look again at the last line of the newspaper article. Explain why you think the writer has chosen to end the article in this way and how it might affect the readers.**

Sample answer

The last line leaves the reader with a positive feeling about the world and the possible relationships within it, however odd and unusual they might be.

7.1 'The discovery of X-rays' by R. A. Gregory, 1896

Basic reading skills

1 **In the first paragraph, the writer names two other scientific advances apart from the discovery of X-rays. List both of these advances.**

Galileo and his use of the telescope; the use of the microscope.

2 **Are the following statements true or false?**

A. Professor Röntgen works at Marburg University. True
B. He has been unable to take photographs using X-rays. False
C. X-rays travel through flesh more easily than bone. True
D. The writer thinks X-rays will help doctors and surgeons. True

3 **The writer refers to 'shadowgraphs'. Based on your understanding of the text, write a definition for this term.**

Shadowgraphs – pictures on a photographic plate that pick up objects that are impermeable to electric rays

4 **Look again at the final paragraph.**

a Name one development that the writer predicts X-rays will helpfully be used for.

In surgery, these pictures will illustrate the nature of fractures.

b Name one development that the writer does not expect X-rays to be used for.

Photographing people's skeletons as they walk along the street.

Advanced reading skills

1 **Look again at the first sentence of the article: 'Science advances by bringing into view facts and phenomena previously unknown.' Explain why you think the writer has chosen to begin the article with this sentence. Do you think it is an effective opening? Give reasons for your answer.**

Sample answer

I think the writer opens the article with this sentence because it is hinting that what is about to be revealed will advance scientific knowledge, thereby whetting the reader's appetite for more information. It is also an effective beginning because it opens up the concepts of viewing and seeing, which are fitting for an article about the development of visual images.

2 **Look again at the opening paragraph.**

a Pick out three quotations that refer to sight or seeing.

'bringing into view'; 'unaided vision'; 'an unseen universe'

b Explain why you think the writer has chosen to include these references.

Sample answer

I think the writer includes these references because they are all linked to sight and what we can see. This introduces the concept of vision, which is exactly what the new invention of 'shadowgraphs' focuses on, although it is a vision of internal objects rather than external ones.

3 **In the first paragraph, the journalist writes: 'It has been discovered that a kind of light-rays – if the term be not a misnomer – can be produced which will pass through opaque substances...'. Explain why the choice of the word 'misnomer' is an appropriate one.**

'Misnomer' is an appropriate word because it means 'unsuitable name'. In fact these electric 'light rays' actually form a picture by producing shadows of opaque materials, and shadows are usually dark, rather than light.

4 **Read the following student's comment on the text:**

The writer is impressed by Professor Röntgen's discovery.

Explain whether you agree or disagree with this statement. Refer to evidence from the text to support your view.

Sample answer

I think the writer is impressed by this discovery because he can foresee the huge advantages that this type of imaging can bring, for example, detecting fractures or deformities in bones and in metal objects. He knows that this imaging has already been used to see 'destroyed parts in a diseased thigh-bone' and 'a stone in the bladder of a living person'. He is confident that 'full advantage' can be taken of this new method of seeing things.

5 **Look at the first and final paragraphs of the article. What links can you find between these two paragraphs, and what effect do these create?**

The first and paragraphs are linked because the first paragraph explains that science moves forward by revealing new facts and things, and the final paragraphs explains how this new invention will literally reveal new things, such as internal structures that are invisible to the naked eye. This brings the structure of the article full circle, proving that this new discovery is a scientific advance.

6 **If you were writing this article for a magazine today, how would you make the text more interesting for a modern-day reader? Think about:**

- **the information presented and the language used to convey this**
- **your choice of sentence forms and the way you could structure the article.**

Rewrite the article in a shorter, more direct way.

Answers will vary.

7.2 'Testing the first atomic bomb' by Richard Feynman, 1985

Basic reading skills

1 **How far away was Richard Feynman from the test site when the atomic bomb was tested?**

20 miles

2 **How close does Richard Feynman say other people were to the test site?**

6 miles

3 **Why does Richard Feynman decide not to wear dark glasses to watch the test?**

He thinks he won't be able to see anything.

4 **What does Richard Feynman do to protect his eyes?**

He gets behind a vehicle's windshield because he thinks the glass will protect him from the ultraviolet light.

5 **'I'm probably the only guy who saw it with the human eye.' List two facts that Richard Feynman gives to support this statement.**

Everyone else wore dark glasses; those who were closest were told to lie on the floor.

6 **Which of the following events seems to prompt the people watching the test to start talking?**

The sound of the bang

7 **Summarize how Bob Wilson appears to feel about the atomic bomb.**

The writer describes Bob Wilson as 'moping' which implies he was unhappy and dwelling on something. He believes they have made something 'terrible'. He appears to feel regret, maybe guilt and a sense of foreboding.

Advanced reading skills

1 **Which of these words best summarizes how Richard Feynman feels during the events of the extract? Write a sentence explaining your choice.**

Sample answer

I think Richard Feynman feels 'excited' during the events because he mentions parties, running around and beating drums.

2 **What do you learn about Richard Feynman? Use a spider diagram to record any clues about his personality and character from the extract.**

Information presented might include:

- independent (didn't do as he was advised)
- clever (he was part of a top science team)
- thinks for himself (decided the screen would give him enough protection)
- curious (wanted to see the explosion directly)
- proud (pleased with the success of the bomb)
- likes a challenge (got caught up in the excitement of the development; didn't think too much about the consequences).

3 **Read the section from the paragraph beginning, 'Time comes...' to the paragraph ending '... the solidity of sound at that distance meant that it had really worked'. Create a timeline to chart the progress of the test explosion. Pick out any quotations that you think are particularly effective in helping you to understand the different stages of the explosion and record these on your timeline.**

Quotations for timeline might include:

- 'tremendous flash'
- 'white light changing'
- 'clouds form and disappear'
- 'big ball of orange'
- 'big ball of smoke with flashes'
- 'tremendous noise - BANG'

4 **Richard Feynman was known as a great communicator, helping non-scientists to understand scientific theories and achievements. How effectively do you think he explains the test explosion of the first atomic bomb?**

Sample answer

I think Feynman is effective in explaining the test explosion because he uses an informal, conversational style of language, which puts the non-scientific reader at ease and conveys a sense of friendliness. His use of phrases such as 'you know', 'you see' and 'and so on', add to the colloquial style of writing, and the contractions such as 'you're' and 'it's' make the writing feel very informal.

The use of direct speech gives the account an immediacy and sense of reality. The reader imagines they are actually there, mingling with the other witnesses, who make very believable, straightforward comments. The use of the present tense in recounting the explosion also helps to add drama to the events and sustain the excitement. If it were all told in the past tense, the reader wouldn't have the same sense of expectation and wonder as events were recounted.

The use of the simile describing the noise of the explosion 'like thunder' is very down to earth and accessible. Although the explosion is unique, he describes it in terms that the reader can understand easily. The image of the orange ball of fire, rising, billowing, blackening and so on is very vivid, giving an extremely clear picture for the reader. Feynman also uses metaphor effectively. He says that the sound of the explosion 'released' everyone, meaning their silence and tension is broken, rather than any sort of literal release. This metaphor is effective in conveying the impression of the spectators being entranced and fascinated by what they are witnessing - almost frozen into silence and completely awestruck.

7.3 'Questioning the universe' by Stephen Hawking, 2008

Basic reading skills

1 **One of the questions Professor Stephen Hawking says he wants to talk about is, 'How did the universe come into being?'**

a List four more questions Professor Stephen Hawking says he wants to talk about.

Where did we come from? Are we alone in the universe? Is there alien life? What is the future of the human race?

b Which of these questions interests you the most? Give a reason for your answer.

Sample answer

I think the most interesting question is what is the future of the human race, because that concerns all of us, including our descendants.

2 **How long ago does Professor Stephen Hawking say the universe began?**

15 billion years ago

3 **Pick out two pieces of evidence Professor Stephen Hawking gives to support his statement that we don't seem to have been visited by aliens.**

He says it's odd that aliens would only appear to 'cranks and weirdos'. The SETI project has not identified any aliens.

4 **List two reasons Professor Stephen Hawking gives to support his claim that we are entering an increasingly dangerous period in our history.**

He says population growth and our use of finite resources threatens life on Earth, but also our aggressive, selfish genetic code means we are a danger to ourselves.

5 **What does Professor Stephen Hawking suggest is the best way to ensure the long-term survival of the human race?**

To look outwards and spread into space.

Advanced reading skills

1 **Why do you think Professor Stephen Hawking includes so many questions in his talk? Support your explanation with examples of questions from the text.**

Sample answer

I think Hawking includes questions in order to help structure his talk. His questions act like headings, which he then goes on to answer in paragraphs. For example, 'where did we come from? How did the universe come into being? Are we alone?' These questions are big ones that most people consider at some point in their lives and by voicing these at the start of his speech, Hawking will engage a lot of people's curiosity.

2 **Look at the structure of the talk. In the opening paragraph Professor Stephen Hawking sets out the five questions he wants to talk about. Copy and complete a table like the one below to record which questions he explores in each paragraph.**

Paragraph	Question explored
2	Where are we from? How did the universe come into being?
3	Are we alone?
4	Are we alone?
5	Is there alien life out there?
6	What is the future of the human race?
7	What is the future of the human race?

3 **Professor Stephen Hawking's talk includes some big ideas. How effectively do you think he explains these for his audience?**

Sample answer

I think Hawking explains his ideas very effectively. His use of questions focuses the audience on each topic he wants to talk about, and he then explores them in more detail. This gives the talk a clear structure which is easy to follow and remember.

The language that he uses to present his ideas is accessible and clear. He tries to give balanced viewpoints so that all aspects of an issue are considered. This is shown by his use of linking phrases and words such as 'on the other hand', 'furthermore', 'but' and 'if'. He refers to possibilities and draws conclusions logically, using terms such as 'this probably indicates' and 'it seems to have been', which reinforces the sense that all his views have been very carefully thought out.

The paragraphs of the talk are linked with words that connect with previous ideas and topics. He opens his paragraphs stating the next step in a sequence of ideas, for example, 'I now turn to the second big question' and 'This brings me to the last of the big questions'. He sometimes opens a new paragraph in order to present another side to an argument, for example, 'On the other hand', 'But we don't know'. These links between the paragraphs glue the ideas together into a logical sequence, making the flow of the ideas coherent and easy to understand.

4 **Read the following student's comment on the text:**

Professor Hawking sounds so clever and this helps to convince you that what he's saying is right.

Do you agree or disagree with this statement? Refer to evidence from the text to support your view.

Sample answer

I agree that Professor Hawking is convincing in his ideas, but I don't think that he makes a conscious effort to 'sound so clever', because he doesn't use particularly complicated vocabulary or sentence structures; in fact the language he uses to explain his thought processes is remarkably clear and accessible, so will appeal to a wide audience, whether they are scientifically trained or not. Maybe this in itself is a sign of 'cleverness' - being able to communicate with a diverse spectrum of people.

5 **If you were asking Professor Stephen Hawking to give this same talk to an audience of primary school children, what changes would you advise him to make to appeal to this younger audience? Rewrite paragraph two as a guide.**

Changes might include:

- simpler vocabulary
- shorter, simpler sentences
- fewer paragraphs
- fewer main questions
- more direct address to the audience
- perhaps more interactive questions (rather than rhetorical ones).

8.1 Grasmere journal by Dorothy Wordsworth, 1802

Basic reading skills

1 **Look again at the first two sentences of the extract.**

a What does Dorothy Wordsworth say the weather is like in Grasmere on Friday 16 April 1802?

The sun shone and the wind had died down.

b What do you think the weather has been like on the previous day? Pick out a quotation that suggests this.

Windy and cloudy. She refers to the 'change' in the weather.

2 **Pick out the quotation that suggests that the first bridge that Dorothy Wordsworth sees is an old bridge.**

'there is a look of ancientry in the architecture'

3 **When Dorothy Wordsworth is resting on the grass and looking back at the bridge, what happens to make a sheep cross the river to the side where she is sitting?**

A little dog on the opposite bank barks at the sheep.

4 **William Wordsworth begins writing a poem while they are on their walk. What does Dorothy Wordsworth say this poem is about?**

The poem is about what they could see and hear around them.

5a **List three features of the landscape described by Dorothy Wordsworth that give you the impression this is a peaceful environment.**

'gentle flowing' stream; 'without a living creature to be seen'; 'a dog barking now and again'

5b **Pick out the quotation which you think gives this impression most effectively and explain your choice.**

Sample answer

'green fields without a living creature to be seen' – The green fields are completely empty, giving an impression of a big expanse of open land, uncluttered by animals, people or machinery.

6a **Create a map to show Dorothy and William Wordsworth's walk. You could refer to an actual map of the area around Grasmere to help you to mark the route of their journey.**

Maps will vary.

6b **Mark on your map the different sights that they saw, picking out relevant quotations from the text to help you to do this.**

Relevant sights might include:

- hills
- river
- Rydale Lake
- valley
- woody knolls
- two-arched bridge
- path
- green fields
- hamlet
- green vale
- Kirkstone
- Ambleside
- Brothers Water.

Advanced reading skills

1 **Dorothy Wordsworth describes passing two sisters who are working in the countryside and writes, 'They laughed long after we were gone, perhaps half in wantonness, half boldness.' Using your own ideas and words, explain why Dorothy Wordsworth thinks they were laughing.**

Sample answer

I think Dorothy's description of the girls laughing 'half in wantonness' implies that they are laughing perhaps for no real reason, just because they are happy and feeling light-hearted – perhaps nowadays we might describe them as giggling. 'Half boldness' implies they are being slightly cheeky, perhaps even laughing at Dorothy and her brother.

2 **This extract is taken from Dorothy Wordsworth's private journal. Note down three features that suggest this.**

Sample answer

She does not use paragraphs and her sentences are fragmented, often just a sequence of phrases to remind her of what she sees and hears and feels. This is as if the journal is never intended for anyone else to read, but just as a brief record of the impressions of the walk. Perhaps she intended her notes to help her later when she incorporates some of these impressions into her poetry.

3 **Dorothy Wordsworth was a poet as well as a writer of prose.**

a Look at the following extract from her journal entry and comment on how her use of language here is poetic:

'Its fleece dropped a glittering shower under its belly. Primroses by the road-side, pile wort that shone like stars of gold in the sun, violets, strawberries, retired and half-buried among the grass.'

Sample answer

The language is poetic because it uses very vivid imagery, such as the metaphor of a 'glittering shower' formed by the river-water droplets. The use of the simile describing the pile wort 'like stars of gold in the sun' enhances the picture of the flowers, glowing and glimmering in the daylight as if they are valuable and rare like gold. The description of the violets and strawberries as 'retired' and 'half-buried' makes them sound modest and secluded, as if they have some shy human characteristics.

b Pick out your own quotation that you think best suggests the poetic nature of Dorothy Wordsworth's language choices. Explain the effects that this quotation creates.

Sample answer

The 'glittering shower' under the fleece best suggests the poetic nature of Dorothy Wordsworth's language, because it conjures up a magical, glamorous image, which in reality is just bits of water from a muddy river, dropping from what was probably a fairly grubby raggedy fleece under the sheep.

4 **Read what this student says about the text:**

Dorothy Wordsworth's writing conveys her love of the countryside.

a Copy the table below. Identify quotations which could support this student's statement. The first one has been done for you.

Quotation
'I was much affected by the beauty of the prospect'
'the hills looked cheerful'
'I was delighted with what I saw'
'the exquisite beauty of the path'

b Choose one quotation from your table and explain how it conveys Dorothy Wordsworth's love of the countryside.

Sample answer

'I was much affected by the beauty of the prospect' conveys the effect that the lovely scenery had on the author. 'Much affected' suggests that it provoked an emotional reaction from her, perhaps almost making her feel tearful at the 'beauty' of the colours and naturally balanced arrangement of the landscape.

5 **What impression do you get of Dorothy Wordsworth's feelings about the places she sees and passes on her walk?**

Sample answer

I get the impression that Dorothy Wordsworth is enchanted by all that she experiences while out on her walk. All her senses are stimulated by her surroundings, for example, she mentions lots of colours, 'green fields', 'grey cottage', 'yellow palms', 'purple and green twigs', and describes the different levels of light at different times of the day and on different objects, for example, the garden 'looked pretty in the half-moonlight, half-daylight'; Rydal Lake had 'its own evening brightness', the ash trees have 'glittering stems'.

She uses similes to convey startling scenes and ideas to the reader, for example, she describes crows becoming 'white as silver' as they flew in the sunshine. This is an unusual description because crows are actually black, and some people associate them with doom and death. She goes on to extend the simile, saying the flock 'looked like shapes of water passing over the green fields', thereby creating a sense of the oozing, fluid movement that the flock create as they move in unison through the sky.

Dorothy's sense of hearing is very acute; she notices how country noises mingle to make up a natural, gentle orchestra that accompanies the astonishing physical beauty of the countryside. She mentions a dog barking, cocks crowing, birds twittering and sisters laughing. These sounds are non-intrusive so she can repeat the words of the poem 'The Glow-worm' as she walks along.

8.2 'The summit of Scafell Pike' by Alfred Wainwright, 1960

Basic reading skills

1 **Re-read the opening paragraph. Pick out three brief quotations that suggest the importance of Scafell Pike.**

'place of many ceremonies and celebrations'; 'the one objective above all others'; 'the supreme'

2 **Now re-read the second paragraph. Why does the writer suggest Scafell Pike attracts so many visitors?**

Because it is the highest ground in England.

3 **Which two of the following things can you find at Scafell Pike?**

An Ordnance Survey triangulation column; a patch of grass

4 **Re-read the following quotation: 'The surrounding area is barren'.**

Pick out two other quotations that give this impression.

'a tumbled wilderness of stones'; 'this rough and desolate summit'

Advanced reading skills

1a **Which of the following words do you think best describe the writer's feelings towards Scafell Pike?**

Proud

1b **Pick out a quotation that best suggests this feeling.**

'This is the summit of England, and it is fitting that it should be sturdy and rugged and strong.'

2 **Re-read the opening paragraph. Comment on how the writer's use of sentence forms conveys an impression of the place he is writing about.**

Sample answer

Wainwright uses one extended sentence which contains many different clauses. It consists of a list of why the summit is important introduced by a colon, but with items separated by semi-colons to make the division of items clear. The list technique builds up a crescendo of praise and superlatives, which is fitting when describing the highest peak in England. He also includes a pun, describing it as an objective 'above all others', with the word 'above' being used both metaphorically and literally. He also uses alliteration to pepper the text with repeated sounds, for example, 'ceremonies/celebrations' and 'bonfires/birthday parties'.

3 **Read what this student says about the description of Scafell Pike.**

The writer makes it sound like a desolate place, devoid of any attractions.

Can you identify any quotations to support this statement? Explain your choices.

Sample answer

Wainwright describes the summit as 'barren' which implies that it is lifeless, lacking in energy and vitality. He also describes it as a 'tumbled wilderness' which suggests it is untidy in a random, cluttered way.

4 **Now re-read the final paragraph. How does the impression the writer gives you of Scafell Pike change here?**

Sample answer

In the final paragraph, Wainwright judges the appearance of the summit to be suitable and appropriate for its status as the 'summit of England'. He doesn't condemn it for its rugged strength, but feels it is an excellent reflection of qualities that represent England.

5 **What overall impression do you get of Scafell Pike from this extract?**

Sample answer

The overall impression I get of Scafell Pike is one of a wild, remote, rugged place, which is popular with visitors (a 'magnet') but still exists in its natural raw state, rather than having been transformed into a scenic public 'promenade'. The 'crumbling' cairn is suitably large for the mountain's status as the highest in England, but it has obviously been buffeted by the elements and is in a state of decay. Although the summit is 'rough and desolate' it does provide a 'patch of grass' for weary walkers to rest on. The writer seems proud of the summit - he likes the fact that it is plain and timeless, he believes it is a 'fitting' scene for the peak.

8.3 *The Old Ways* by Robert Macfarlane, 2013

Basic reading skills

1 **At what time of day does Robert Macfarlane begin the journey described in the extract?**

Just after dawn

2 **Summarize the accident that Robert Macfarlane has on the early part of his journey.**

Sample answer

The accident occurred on the Roman road, near the Iron Age ring-fort. As the writer was cycling fast downhill the front wheel hit hard soil, the bike twisted and he crashed into the handlebars. His injuries included pain in his ribs, a bleeding elbow and a lump on his kneecap, as well as damage to his self-respect.

3 **When Robert Macfarlane describes his accident to a friend, he is told: 'This was an entry fee to the old way, charged at one of the usual tollbooths. Now you can proceed. You're in. Bone for chalk: you've paid your due.' Using your own words, explain what his friend means by this.**

Sample answer

The friend means that the injuries were the price that the writer had to pay in order to pursue the rest of the ride. He likens the price to that of a tollbooth, where in the past people had to pay money to gain access to the way.

4 **Robert Macfarlane is following in the footsteps of Edward Thomas, a poet and journalist who walked the Icknield Way in 1911. List two facts about Edward Thomas that you can find from the text.**

Edward Thomas wrote an account of his journey along the Way; he suffered badly from depression.

5 **List three different things that Robert Macfarlane hears on his journey.**

Animals in a nearby zoo; the roar of traffic; the hum of pylons.

6 **Robert Macfarlane writes: 'The landscape's emptiness spooked me'.**

a Pick out two quotations that you think best describe the emptiness of the landscape.

'an evacuated landscape'; 'post-apocalypse'

b Now re-read the final two paragraphs. Pick out three details that suggest he is leaving this emptiness behind.

'the roar of the cars'; 'the song of the pylons'; 'chirruping' parakeets in cages

Advanced reading skills

1 **Choose one word from the list below that best describes the mood created by this extract. Explain your choice of word.**

The mood seems 'contemplative' as the writer notices details of the natural world around him and reflects on the area's history.

2 **Re-read the paragraph beginning, 'Quickly I was onto the chalky field-edge footpaths...'. How does the writer build a picture of the setting here?**

Sample answer

The writer builds up a vivid picture of the setting by describing what he sees and hears. He describes going through a 'tunnel of spindle and hawthorn', conveying the image of a tubular enclosure made out of vegetation. The adjective 'narrow' gives the feeling of quite a restricted place. He describes the light as 'pearled' on the barley crop, suggesting an iridescence that signifies something of great value. The white flowers create an image like 'foam' on the hawthorn hedges, conveying a sense of burgeoning fertility and natural generosity. The writer also focuses on the sounds that he hears: 'pigeons clattered' and 'skylarks pelted their song down', as if showering the writer in their profusion. The short sentence forms give the effect of a list of observations and feelings, as the writer settles into the walk as 'the shock of the crash began to fade away'. It is as though the writer is finding his rhythm as a walker, as well as a sense of stability again.

3 **In the text the writer describes his own experience of following the Icknield Way, but also writes about other people such as Edward Thomas and John Emslie who have walked this route.**

a Re-read the text to identify the paragraphs where the writer focuses on the experiences and views of other people.

Paragraphs 2, 5, 6 and 7

b Why do you think the writer has chosen to include these other views of the Icknield Way?

Sample answer

I think the writer chooses to include these other views of the Icknield Way because they prove that this route has been important for many people. Not only is it an ancient historic route, but people also read into it a greater significance, giving it a mythic, almost magical, power. He describes it as 'a path that stood as a prototype for all others' and which took people all round the world and back to where they started, like the mythical serpent 'uroboros' whose tail led back into its mouth. The writer also mentions that for one author, Thomas, his account of walking this path was also a record of his terrible depression, suggesting that the way might have some therapeutic qualities. Thomas also believed that every traveller would be adding his or her own dreams to those that had gone before and that somehow they would lie in layers beneath people's feet. This suggests that the author might believe that he is somehow contributing to the history of the pathway, giving his journey more significance and weight.

4 **Read what the following student says about the text:**

Robert Macfarlane describes the beauty of the natural world, but also conveys the beauty of the man-made environment too.

Do you agree with this statement? Copy and complete the table below by picking out quotations where the beauty of the natural world and the man-made environment is either explicitly shown or implied. Some examples have been given.

Natural world	Man-made environment
'The scent of dog-rose sweetened the air'	**'the sun-strikes off windscreen and paintwork lent it the distant dazzle of moving water'**
'its wide verges are brocaded with flowers'	'the distant hum of the M11 motorway, growing to a roar'
'a crow flopped from an ash tree, its wings silver with sun'	'a ghostly high carolling, intermittent and tentative... a loose chord'
'a lemony light pushed through the gaps'	'heat-waves rising from the asphalt'
'skylarks pelted their song down'	
'light pearled on barley'	

9.1 *Down and out in Paris and London* by George Orwell, 1933

Basic reading skills

1 **How many shops does the writer visit before he finds one where he is able to sell his clothes?**

Three

2 **George Orwell writes, 'My new clothes had put me instantly in a new world.' Pick out two ways he says people treat him differently when wearing the dirty clothes the shopkeeper gave him.**

A street hawker calls him 'mate'; women shudder away from him.

3 **Why does the writer say he dared not speak to anyone once he was wearing these new clothes?**

He was afraid that people might question the disparity between his accent and his appearance.

4 **Look again at the following extract from the text: 'Dressed in a tramp's clothes it is very difficult, at any rate for the first day, not to feel that you are genuinely degraded. You might feel the same shame, irrational but very real, your first night in prison.'**

Rewrite the sentence in your own way to show what Orwell means. What does the extract suggest about the writer's feelings about his situation?

Sample answer

When you are dressed like a tramp you feel a less worthy human being. It's like being punished for some wrong-doing. This description suggests that the writer feels a sense of injustice and humiliation at the way people react to his tramp's clothes.

5 **List four details about the room that the writer stays in overnight.**

It smelt foul; it was 15 feet square and 8 feet high; there were eight beds in it; the beds were hard and narrow.

Advanced reading skills

1 **Re-read the first three paragraphs of the extract. How does the writer suggest the shopkeeper's attitude towards him?**

Sample answer

The writer suggests that the shopkeeper's attitude was rather condescending towards him. He explains that the shopkeeper felt his clothes 'disparagingly' which suggests that he is judging them to be shoddy and of poor quality, and claims they are 'poor stuff', even though in fact they are of good quality. When the writer asks for some money, the shopkeeper 'pursed his lips' which implies that he puckered them up, as if in disapproval. The fact that he 'threw' the ragged clothes down for the writer, also suggests disdain and a lack of respect. The writer instinctively starts to argue to defend himself, but when he sees that the shopkeeper is likely to take back the shilling, he decides to say nothing, knowing that he is 'helpless' in the situation.

2 **Re-read the following sentence:**

'I had worn bad enough things before, but nothing at all like these; they were not merely dirty and shapeless, they had—how is one to express it?—a gracelessness, a patina of antique filth, quite different from mere shabbiness.'

How effective is this sentence in giving you an impression of the writer's new clothes?

Sample answer

This sentence is made up of many clauses and uses many different forms of punctuation to link the different parts: comma, semi-colon, dashes for parenthesis and question mark to show a rhetorical question. By structuring the sentence like this, the writer conveys the impression of a man trying to explain carefully and in detail the depth of grime on the clothes and the repulsion that he feels towards them. The rhetorical question acts like a pause, as he thinks of a way to convey his reaction to the hideous clothes. The phrase 'a patina of antique filth' conjures up an image of a thin layer of grime, cleverly contrasting with the usual use of the word 'patina' which means a glossy finish created by polish, usually on wood. The fact that the filth is 'antique' implies that it isn't just recently acquired dirt, but has accumulated in layers over years.

3 **How does the writer's use of direct speech suggest how his situation has changed? Referring to the text, comment on what the direct speech suggests about the people the writer encounters.**

Sample answer

The use of direct speech to relay the shopkeeper's reaction to the writer's clothes gives a sense of immediacy and conveys the rather abrupt, unsympathetic attitude he has. There are no 'niceties' in this speech. No greeting, or hint of friendliness.

The way that the hawker addresses the writer as 'mate' is significant because the writer has never been called this before, presumably because he has always been regarded as too 'posh' and formal, but now the hawker is judging him to be a social equal to himself, so he is a 'mate' rather than 'sir'.

The direct speech of the navvy and the tired boy convey the sense of poverty and lack of education. The contracted words, for example, 'ouse' and 'gov'nor' give the passage a colloquial feel, conveying the real sound of street talk. Both the navvy and the boy are helpful towards the writer, but they don't waste words on unnecessary pleasantries.

4 **Re-read the extract and answer the following questions.**

a Copy and complete the following table to identify how the writer uses different senses to describe his experience.

Touch	Smell	Hearing	Sight
'the bed... was as hard as a board'	'a sweetish reek of paregoric and foul linen'	'noisily used his chamber pot'	'a grey, sunken face like that of a corpse'
'a mere hard cylinder like a block of wood'	'stank so horribly of sweat'	'swore vilely'	'his trousers wrapped round his head'
'mattress was convex'	'stuffy'	'coughing fit'	'bed was not six feet long and very narrow'
		'a foul bubbling and retching'	

b Choose the sensory detail that you find most effective and explain how it helps you to imagine the writer's experience.

Sample answer

The phrase 'a grey, sunken face like that of a corpse' suggests to me that the writer is staying in a place with people so desperate and poor that they are just waiting to die, and physically on the verge of death.

5 **How does the writer's use of language help to give you an impression of how unpleasant he finds his situation throughout the extract?**

Sample answer

The writer's careful choice of vocabulary and phrasing convey very detailed impressions of what he witnesses and experiences. The description of other people's reactions to him imply that he has sunk down the social order and feels humiliated and unfairly judged. His use of direct speech creates a realistic insight into the characters he encounters and gives the reader an idea of the tone and attitudes that they present.

The writer describes his situation in the lodgings through all his senses, creating a very strong impression of the revulsion and horror that he experiences. The words used to describe the smells, such as 'reek', 'stank' and 'foul', make the reader want to gag, and the sounds conjure up images of illness and unpleasant private bodily functions. He admits the sounds were 'unspeakably repellent' and goes on to suggest that the man's bowels were disturbed, relaying a distasteful image in the reader's mind.

The writer uses mainly multi-clause sentences so that he can string together lots of details as he describes what he witnesses. The occasional use of simple sentences helps to break up the text. For example, in the final paragraph he states, 'Several noises recurred throughout the night' then proceeds to describe them in detailed, multi-clause sentences. The other simple sentences are in the direct speech, which gives the impression of people not wanting to waste words, or not having the skills to construct more complicated sentences.

9.2 'A nightly scene in London' by Charles Dickens, 1856

Basic reading skills

1 **Re-read the opening paragraph.**

a What part of London does Charles Dickens find himself in?

Whitechapel

b Pick out the quotation that suggests he didn't intend to visit this part of London.

'accidentally strayed'

2 **Look again at the paragraph beginning, 'Crouched against the wall of the Workhouse...'. Using your own words, summarize what Charles Dickens sees outside the workhouse.**

Five bundles of rags – actually people.

3a **List three things Charles Dickens compares the figures he sees outside the workhouse to.**

Beehives; dead bodies; bundles of rags

3b **What impression do these comparisons give you of Dickens' feelings towards the figures? Give reasons for your answer.**

Sample answer

Dickens feels revulsion and horror towards the figures, but also sympathy. The beehives comparison suggests that there is a lot of buzzing around the bundles, perhaps flies attracted to the dirt and smell of them. The comparison with dead bodies suggests they are still and decaying, something that Dickens wouldn't like to touch. The description of them as bundles of rags makes the people sound like refuse or cast-offs that society has neglected, implying some sympathy from Dickens.

4 **Why does Charles Dickens decide to speak to the master of the workhouse? Choose the correct statement from the list below.**

He wants to find out if the women outside the workhouse are thieves.

5 **Why have the women been refused entry to the casual ward of the workhouse?**

Because the ward is full.

6 **Which of the following groups of people does the master of the workhouse say are given preference?**

B. women with children.

7 **Re-read the final paragraph.**

a What does Charles Dickens do to help the woman?

He gives her a shilling.

b How does the woman respond to Dickens' help?

She gets up and moves away without thanking him.

Advanced reading skills

1 **Choose one word from the list below that best describes Dickens' feelings about the 'nightly scene' he describes in his article. Explain your choice of word.**

Sample answer

I think 'shocked' best describes Dickens' feelings about the scene because he has difficulty understanding what the bundles are to begin with; he is quite horrified that they are actually people. He feels compelled to find out more about the 'bundles' and to try to help at least one of them.

2 **Read what the following student says about the description of the figures Dickens sees outside the workhouse.**

The way the figures are described makes it seem as if they aren't even human.

Can you identify any evidence to support this statement?

Sample answer

The figures are described as 'ragged mounds' and compared with beehives, corpses and static Sphinxes. This comparison with inanimate things conveys the stillness of the people, their lack of life and energy.

3 **Charles Dickens tells the master of the workhouse: 'I don't blame you. I may find fault with the system you administer'. Find evidence from the text that suggests Dickens blames society for the situation he witnesses. Explain your choices.**

Sample answer

Dickens states that the ragged mounds seem to question what will happen to 'society that leaves us here'. The other observer comments that it is an awful sight to witness 'in a Christian country'. Dickens reassures the master of the workhouse that he does not blame him personally for the lack of care for the people and acknowledges that the preference given to women with children is the most humane way of deciding who gets the limited shelter available.

4 **Re-read the final section of the extract from the paragraph beginning, 'We went to the ragged bundle nearest to the Workhouse-door...'.**

a Pick out one example of dialogue that you think best indicates the time the article was written. Explain your choice.

Sample answer

The woman explains that she was at the workhouse 'the night afore too'. The use of the word 'afore' suggests that the article was written in an earlier era, as nowadays we don't use the word 'afore', we would be more likely to say 'before'.

b What impression do you get of the homeless woman from this section?

Sample answer

The impression I get of the homeless woman in this section is of a person with no energy and no expectations. She is reluctant to emerge from her rags, perhaps she has sunk into a depression or is overcome with lethargy due to hunger and thirst. She may also be ill. She seems to have lost faith and hope in people, because she doesn't really engage with Dickens or his companion. She won't look at them as they talk, just gazes around her, listlessly. It is as if she has very low expectations of what might happen. Although the woman answers Dickens and shows her emaciated neck to him, she never thanks him for giving her the money or says goodbye. It is as if she is barely conscious of what is happening and is beyond valuing human interaction. There is a feeling of complete hopelessness about her.

c 'I have seen many strange things, but not one that has left a deeper impression on my memory that the dull impassive way in which that worn-out heap of misery took that piece of money, and was lost.' What does this sentence suggest about how the experience has affected Dickens?

Sample answer

This sentence suggests that this incident affected Dickens profoundly. It has obviously stuck in his mind and he can recount it in great detail. The description of the young woman as 'that worn-out heap of misery' sums up how desperate and dehumanizing real poverty is. She has lost all personal identity and character, and Dickens feels that she is entirely 'lost'.

9.3 'The Foodbank Dilemma' by James Harrison, 2014

Basic reading skills

1 **In the storeroom the writer says he sees 'numbers scrawled in black highlighter pen everywhere'. What information do these numbers give?**

The numbers are the use-by dates, when the foods should be eaten by.

2a **List the names of three supermarkets who collect food for the foodbank.**

Tesco, Morrisons and Sainsbury's

2b **Name one other type of place where people donate food to the foodbank.**

Churches

3 **The writer describes two men, one young and one old, waiting to use the foodbank. When asked who referred them to the foodbank, 'the younger man says gruffly, "It's not for me, it's for my dad."' What does this suggest about how the younger man feels about using the foodbank?**

He is embarrassed and feels awkward about being there.

4 **Which of the following statements best describes the role of the foodbank?**

A. To help people with short-term crises.

5 **Re-read the paragraph beginning, 'Hugh asks me if I want to meet some of the clients.'**

a Using your own words, explain why the writer isn't sure about meeting some of the people who use the foodbank.

Sample answer

He is unsure about meeting people who use the foodbank because he might be intruding on something that is rather private and people might feel sensitive about it.

b What convinces the writer to meet some of the clients?

He sees a journalist and photographer talking to people and asking for pictures.

c Look again at the sentence, 'I steel myself and agree to Hugh's offer.' What does the word 'steel' mean in this context?

The word 'steel' here means to strengthen your resolve, to be tough and face up to whatever you want to do.

6 **Give three factors that have led Louise to use the foodbank.**

Loss of some of her allowances; delay of payout for her appeal; the school holidays

7 **Select a quotation that you think best suggests Louise's gratitude towards the foodbank. Explain your choice of quotation.**

'Louise's eyes light up'. This quotation shows the pleasure and thankfulness that Louise feels towards the foodbank. It is a spontaneous, undisguised reaction that is more powerful than words.

Advanced reading skills

1 **What do you think the writer's view of foodbanks is? Support your opinion with reference to the text.**

Sample answer

I think that the writer believes that foodbanks provide much-needed support to people who are in a crisis situation. The final sentence refers to 'the feeling of joy we all felt when her food arrived' which suggests that everyone, including the writer himself, was pleased that the foodbank was able to help Louise.

2 **Look at the following student's statement:**

People only use foodbanks to get free food, not because they can't afford to eat.

a Find three pieces of evidence from the text to challenge this point of view.

Sample answer

People have to be referred to the foodbank by agencies, for example, schools, hospitals, GP surgeries, which means they have been assessed as being in need. People can't just walk in off the streets and take the free food. The entitlement to the foodbank is also rationed: everyone is entitled to three vouchers over a six-month period, so they can't come whenever they want. The article shows that people use the foodbank reluctantly; they are driven by need, not by the desire for free food.

b Look at the pieces of evidence you have identified and select the one that you think would be the most effective in changing this student's mind. Give reasons for your choice.

Sample answer

The fact that people have to be referred to the foodbank by other agencies proves that people aren't just after free food. They have been identified by responsible, sympathetic organizations to be in real need or at a crisis point.

3 **How does the way the writer uses language to describe the users of the foodbank influence your responses as a reader to them? Explore the use of language in the following sentences:**

'A young clean-shaven man leads an older, grey-haired, battered-by-life-version-of-himself to where Tony stands.'

Sample answer

The writer describes the two men as being 'young' and 'old' respectively, explaining that they could be the same person, but at different stages of life. The older man is 'battered-by-life' which means he has obviously undergone hardship and maybe disappointment, and this shows in him physically. The description of 'clean-shaven' suggests that the younger man takes care of himself, and we are told he is leading the older man, which suggests that he is the more confident and more physically able of the two. The 'older, grey-haired' man we imagine as being more frail and dependent on the younger man. The multi-clause sentence contains noun phrases to describe each of the men in turn, but concludes with the arrival of Tony.

'He approaches a small, slight young woman, who is sitting crumpled and small on a chair in the corner.'

Sample answer

In this description the repetition of 'small' reinforces the sense of vulnerability and fragility of the woman. The fact that she is 'young' and 'slight' further suggests that she is rather thin and in need of help. The word 'crumpled' conveys the impression of both literally crumpled clothes – perhaps her iron is broken, or she doesn't possess one – and also a rather chaotic life, in which she is always rushed and not able to sort things out for herself. The fact that she is sitting in a chair in the corner implies that she is isolated, perhaps shy, and even hints at some sort of old-fashioned punishment because traditionally naughty children were told to stand in a corner of a schoolroom, in front of their classmates in order to highlight their poor behaviour.

4 **Look at the following statement from a student about this text:**

This article is biased and only provides a one-sided view of foodbanks.

Do you agree or disagree with this statement? Find evidence from the text to support your point of view.

Sample answer

I don't think that this article is biased because bias implies the telling of an incomplete story, distorting the truth or hiding some facts. However, this article looks very carefully at the facts regarding who supplies the foodbank (Tesco, Morrisons, Sainsbury's and Costco), who uses a foodbank and how they get access to it (via churches, schools, GPs, social services), and then interviews people who both work at and use the foodbank to back up these facts, for example, the writer talks to a father and son, a single mother, Hugh who runs the foodbank and Tony, the volunteer co-ordinator.

10.1 'Why I hate Shakespeare' by Krystie Lee Yandoli, 2014

Basic reading skills

1a **Re-read the second paragraph. Which book does the writer say she was given at school?**

The Complete Works of William Shakespeare

1b **Now re-read the final paragraph. Why was the writer given this book?**

She was given it as an award while she was a junior student in high school.

2 **Name two adaptations of Shakespeare plays that the writer says she was aware of when she was growing up.**

West Side Story; 10 Things I Hate About You

3a **Identify the name of the first Shakespeare play that the writer studied at school.**

Hamlet

3b **Which of the following reasons does the writer give to explain why she found studying this text difficult?**

A. She found it difficult to understand the language the play was written in.

Pick out the quotation that best supports the reason you have chosen.

'Early Modern English hurt my brain and I couldn't seem to wrap my head around it.'

4 **'I'd rather not put an old, rich, white man from regal Britain and his antiquated ideologies about society on a pedestal.' Explain what this statement means using your own words.**

Sample answer

This statement means that the writer doesn't feel she has to admire a man from the past who was rich, white and had old-fashioned ideas about people and how they should behave.

5 **The writer says, 'I couldn't help but feel insecure about my lack of enthusiasm for Shakespeare.' Pick out two quotations from the text which suggest the writer's insecurity.**

'I fear the judgment and ridicule of others'; 'all I ever wanted in the world is to be taken seriously as a writer and lover of literature, and I never thought that could happen if I admitted to my disdain for Shakespeare.'

Advanced reading skills

1 **Create a timeline showing the writer's encounters with the work of William Shakespeare. On your timeline you should identify:**

- **specific plays the writer is aware of or has studied**
- **when she encountered these plays**
- **any feelings she shares about these.**

Labels on timeline might include:

- Awarded *The Complete Works of William Shakespeare* (in high school)
- *West Side Story*
- *10 Things I Hate About You*
- *Hamlet* (6th grade, 'I was beyond lost')
- *The Taming of the Shrew* ('problematic' and 'unenjoyable')
- *The Tempest* or *Macbeth* ('a knot in my stomach')

2 **Look at the following student's comment about the structure of this blog.**

The way the writer organizes the blog chronologically, taking the reader through her experiences of Shakespeare through school and into her academic career, is very effective. I think this helps to convince the reader to agree with her view of Shakespeare as the evidence to support why she doesn't like him is built up over time.

Do you agree or disagree with this student's comment? Refer to the text to support your point of view.

Sample answer

I think that the chronological structure explaining when and how the writer encountered Shakespeare gives an effective explanation of her attitude towards his work. However, it does not persuade me of her viewpoint, because it seems that the first time she was properly introduced to Shakespeare was when she had to study *Hamlet*. This is one of the longest, most complex of Shakespeare's plays, and highly likely to put any student off if they haven't studied some of the 'easier' plays first, such as *Romeo and Juliet* or *A Midsummer Night's Dream*. The writer then focuses on her experience of reading *The Taming of the Shrew*, which is probably one of the most problematic Shakespeare plays to read nowadays because of the different social attitudes held in Elizabethan times compared with today. Plays such as *King Lear*, *Macbeth* and *Othello* present more universal themes and ideas which do not date. So, although I have some sympathy with the writer's viewpoint - particularly with the trickiness of the language - I am not entirely convinced by her arguments which are linked to the clever structure of the blog.

3 **The writer states, 'I've been encouraged to read and love Shakespeare throughout my life.' Pick out two quotations that show the writer being encouraged to read and love Shakespeare.**

'I had been told time and again that Shakespeare is "the greatest writer of all time"; 'From grade school through higher education, we're all taught to admire the Bard, and there's great shame attached to saying you don't like this literary icon.'

4 **Look at the following quotations and explain how the vocabulary the writer uses to describe Shakespeare helps to convey her negative opinion of him.**

- **'Shakespeare's inherent sexism'**
- **'an old, rich, white man from regal Britain and his antiquated ideologies'**

Sample answer

The choice of the noun phrase 'inherent sexism' is emotive because 'sexism' is widely perceived to be undesirable and at worst damaging and destructive. Many people campaign energetically against sexism, believing it deprives females of the respect and equality that they deserve. The description of Shakespeare as 'an old, rich, white man from regal Britain and his antiquated ideologies' is also very provocative. It suggests that Shakespeare was also racist and royalist, rather than someone who believed that all people were equal and that the privilege of the royals and aristocracy was unearned and therefore immoral. The phrase 'antiquated ideologies' implies that his ideas are out of date and no longer relevant to modern life. The string of adjectives 'old', 'rich', 'white', 'regal' and 'antiquated' all have negative connotations in this context, therefore reinforcing the writer's prejudice against Shakespeare.

5 **Re-read the final three paragraphs of the text. How does the writer convey how her feelings about Shakespeare have changed?**

Sample answer

The writer no longer feels embarrassed about her disdain for Shakespeare. She still feels that he is 'overrated' and has 'come to terms with' her 'unpopular opinion'. She says that coming to terms with her feelings has been a 'long road' meaning that a lot of time has had to pass and she has had to cover a lot of ground before she can be comfortable with her conclusion. As she has grown in confidence, she 'no longer fear[s] the judgment and ridicule of others' and she feels unapologetic about her attitude. Although she still values the book she was given as an award, it is because of its physical beauty encased in a red-velvet cover and with gold-lined pages, rather than because of its contents.

The writer uses a rhetorical question to emphasize her attitude. She asks 'why should I have to force myself to read something that's supposed to be enjoyable?' This honesty gives her argument weight and the reader wonders if perhaps other people feel the same way as the writer, but don't like to admit to it. The use of multi-clause sentences enables the writer to explain in detail her thoughts in a fluid, logical manner. The clauses are linked with conjunctions such as 'because', 'and' and 'but' which express cause and effect, statements and counter-statements. This conveys the impression of a well-thought-out argument that is carefully considered and rational, leading to a logical conclusion.

10.2 *William Shakespeare's Romeo and Juliet* review by Peter Travers, 1996

Basic reading skills

1 **Using the information from the text, create a cast list for *William Shakespeare's Romeo and Juliet*. In the cast list you should include the name of the character and the actor who played them. The first part has been done for you.**

Romeo Leonardo DiCaprio

Juliet Claire Danes

Father Capulet Paul Sorvino

Mother Capulet Diane Venora

Paris Paul Rudd

Nurse Miriam Margolyes

Tybalt John Leguizamo

Father Montague Brian Dennehy

Mother Montague Christina Pickles

Father Laurence Pete Postlethwaite

2 **Why does the writer suggest a viewer might almost laugh watching Leonardo DiCaprio and Claire Danes play the parts of Romeo and Juliet? Pick out a quotation to support your answer.**

The writer suggests that a viewer might almost laugh in 'delight and awe' because DiCaprio and Danes put such a modern, passionate slant on the traditional, classic story. He describes it as 'a hip hotblooded spin on the Bard's star-crossed lovers'.

3 **Look again at the second paragraph. Why might the film be called *Quentin Tarantino's Romeo and Juliet* by mistake? How is this mistake avoided?**

The film uses Quentin Tarantino-type effects in terms of its violence and drama. However, the film couldn't be called *Quentin Tarantino's Romeo and Juliet* because it also includes Elizabethan verse and spirited comedy, while retaining the tragic elements.

4 **Other film adaptations of *Romeo and Juliet* mentioned by the writer include *West Side Story* and *China Girl*. What does the writer say is the key difference between these adaptations and Baz Luhrmann's film?**

The key difference is that these other film adaptations do not use Shakespeare's language.

5a **Copy and complete the following sentence to summarize the writer's feelings about this film.**

Sample answer

I think the reviewer feels the film is an energetic, vibrant, superb retelling of this classic tale, well cast and acted.

5b **Pick out one quotation from the text that you think best illustrates the writer's feelings. Explain your choice of quotation.**

Sample answer

'Luhrmann and his two bright angels have shaken up a 400-year-old play without losing its touching, poetic innocence'. I think this quotation sums up the writer's feelings because it acknowledges that DiCaprio and Danes are at their sparkling best and, with the direction of Luhrmann, they refresh the old play, without losing any of the most delicate, poignant aspects of it.

Advanced reading skills

1 **The adjectives the writer chooses to describe the film he is reviewing can influence a reader's opinion. What impression do the adjectives used in the following quotation give you: 'hip, hotblooded spin on the Bard's star-crossed lovers'?**

The adjectives 'hip' and 'hotblooded' give the impression of something modern, energetic and exciting. This conveys the message that the story is relevant for today's audiences and isn't just a relic revived from the past.

2 **The two lead actors in *William Shakespeare's Romeo and Juliet* are Leonardo DiCaprio and Claire Danes.**

a Copy and complete a table below by picking out quotations where the writer conveys his view about their performances.

Leonardo DiCaprio	Claire Danes
'dynamite'	'poise beyond her years'
'rare talent'	'chooses to emphasize Juliet's melting loveliness and bristling wit'
'when he speaks, you believe him'	'speaks Elizabethan verse with unforced grace'
'DiCaprio lets the Bard's words flow with an ardor that you can't buy in acting class'	'youth to play the roles and the talent to do them justice'

b Choose one quotation from each column of the table and explore how it conveys the writer's view about the selected actor's performance.

Sample answer

The writer says that 'DiCaprio lets the Bard's words flow with an ardor that you can't buy in acting class', meaning that he speaks the Elizabethan verse with a passion that you can't simply teach someone to display. He is implying that the credit is due to DiCaprio's raw, personal talent, rather than something that he has been schooled in.

He admires Danes' choice to 'emphasize Juliet's melting loveliness and bristling wit', meaning that the qualities she presents in her interpretation of the role bring to attention the gentle but powerful beauty of Juliet and her lively mind which enables her to play with words in a humorous way.

3 **What impression do you get of the writer's opinion of this film?**

Sample answer

I get the impression that the writer is extremely impressed by all aspects of this film. He praises the acting given by the two lead roles, describing DiCaprio as displaying 'rare talent' and Danes as showing 'poise beyond her years', meaning that she acts in a mature, sophisticated way for someone so young. The directing is described as innovative and energetic, fulfilling a vision that sets the action in scenes more commonly associated with other types of films, such as action-packed modern urban gangster films. The writer says that Luhrmann 'relishes knocking cobwebs off classics' and succeeds in shaking up 'a 400-year-old play without losing its touching, poetic innocence'. The writer presents his thoughts and feelings very strongly by comparing this adaptation with other productions, pinpointing the weaknesses of previous films and thereby highlighting the strengths of this one. He also mentions the history of many of the actors, linking them to roles that the reader may be more familiar with. This association with other parts helps to give the actors context and the reader can consider their other achievements too. The writer also pre-empts and counters criticism from 'outraged purists' who he obviously feels completely miss the quality and impact of this adaptation, which he feels is powerful as well as sensitive.

4 **Look at the following statement about what a film review should do: 'A good review should help you decide whether it is worth spending money to see a film.'**

Explain whether you think this text is a good review. Refer to evidence from the text to support your answer.

Sample answer

I think this text is a good review because it explains how this is a startlingly fresh, novel and different approach to this classic love story. Describing it as 'a hip, hotblooded spin on the Bard's star-crossed lovers' in the opening paragraph immediately catches the reader's attention and rouses curiosity. The mention of 'laughter' is quite surprising because most people consider this story to be a terrible tragedy, so the reader immediately knows that this production is something very different.

The next paragraph focuses on the setting, which is made to sound so unlikely that the reader again is intrigued. This review might make the film appealing to audiences that wouldn't normally choose to see a film based on a Shakespeare play. The action-packed outline gives the reader a sense of the pace and drama of the story.

The description of the actors, their history and the way they play their parts conveys enough detail to whet the appetite of potential film-goers without giving away too much (although of course the ending is common knowledge). Mention of the costumes and props conjures up vivid images in the reader's mind and the description of Luhrmann as 'a wizard' with 'rabid flamboyance' of vision creates a startling impression of the director's skills.

However, the review also gives hints that some people may not like the adaptation, particularly if they are 'purists', and dislike anything that is not in a traditional context. This gives a clear indication about what sort of people would and wouldn't enjoy the film, which is a valuable quality in a review.

10.3 *Richard II* with Mr Kean, 1825

Basic reading skills

1 **Re-read the first paragraph. Pick out the quotation that suggests that the character of Richard II is a difficult part for an actor to play.**

'the character is heavy in representation, and requires talent of the very highest order'

2 **Look again at the second paragraph. List three features of Edmund Kean's performance that the reviewer praises.**

'exhibited with great force and truth'; 'varied and pointed delivery'; 'high treat to hear the fine language of Shakespeare from the mouth of Kean'

3 **Re-read the third paragraph which describes the performance of the after-piece *Of Age To-Morrow* in which Edmund Kean plays the part of Frederick Baron Willinghurst.**

a Pick out three differences between Edmund Kean's performance of Richard II and his performance of Frederick Baron Willinghurst.

Sample answer

He sang and danced and tumbled (did acrobatics) in the after-piece, but not as Richard II, who had reflective and moralizing parts. As Frederick Baron Willinghurst, he played a comic character in a farce, whereas he played a tragic role as Richard II. There is the suggestion that he performed the role of the baron as much for his own entertainment, as for that of his audience, suggesting that it was a rather self-indulgent performance.

b The reviewer writes: 'The dignity of the great tragedian was put aside for the broadest farce – an experiment of the policy of which we cannot help doubting.' Using your own words, explain what the reviewer thinks about Edmund Kean's performance in the after-piece.

Sample answer

This comment suggests that by juxtaposing the role of the tragic king with the light, funny role of the baron, the importance and impact of the former was diminished. It would have left the audience with a lesser regard for Kean's acting abilities.

4 **Pick out a quotation that suggests the audience enjoyed Edmund Kean's performance.**

Sample answer

After the curtain fall, the audience gave 'a loud and pretty general cry for Mr Kean' to appear and this went on 'for about a quarter of an hour'.

5 **Re-read the final paragraph and summarize what happened when Edmund Kean returned to the stage.**

Mr Kean gave a speech that was 'a pretty considerable quantity of nonsense', in fact so poor that it was not worth the reviewer repeating.

Advanced reading skills

1 **Look again at the opening paragraph of the review. How does this try to hook the reader's interest?**

The first paragraph tries to hook the reader's interest by mentioning 'talent of the very highest order', and Kean's ability to 'keep alive the interest of the piece to the last'. It also mentions that Mr Kean was about to go to America, suggesting that his talents are appreciated worldwide.

2 **Re-read the second paragraph. How does the writer's choice of sentence structure and punctuation here help to convey his opinion of the performance?**

Sample answer

The writer uses two long complex sentences in the second paragraph in order to convey some detailed, appreciative commentary on Mr Kean's performance. The first sentence begins with a very positive main clause, stating the portrayal of the king as being done 'with great force and truth'. Two subordinating clauses follow, introduced by the words 'while' and 'which', giving further detail, including an example of how badly some parts of the role could have been performed. The second sentence in the paragraph begins with a fronted adverbial, starting 'After being accustomed to...', and continues to describe how a monotonous performance means that nothing is told 'forcibly' (that is, it loses its effect). In contrast, the final clause, which is the main clause, states that 'it is a high treat' to hear Mr Kean's presentation of 'the fine language of Shakespeare'. The use of multiple clauses, separated by commas, enables the writer to link a series of observations in order to back up his main statements about the talent of Mr Kean.

3 **Re-read the second paragraph beginning 'The irresolute changeable monarch ...'. Comment on the impression the writer's use of verbs and adjectives give you of his opinion towards Edmund Kean's performance.**

Sample answer

The adjectives 'irresolute' and 'changeable' describe the character of Richard II, implying that he isn't a character who behaves in a consistent manner. This suggests that the actor who plays him requires a great level of skill, and the reviewer's description of his presentation being one of 'great force and truth' is very flattering for Mr Kean. The reviewer says that the 'reflecting and moralizing parts' of the role in the hands of an 'inferior' or less skilled actor could be 'scarcely endurable', but 'Mr Kean's varied and pointed delivery' made it hugely interesting. Instead of having to listen to 'monotonous', boring language, all delivered in the same tone and volume, the variation made the language more interesting and meaningful. The description of Mr Kean's delivery of the 'fine language of Shakespeare' as a 'high treat' is very complimentary to the actor.

4 **Look again at the final paragraph. How does the writer's use of language and sentence forms help to convey how his opinion of Edmund Kean's performance has changed?**

Sample answer

In the final paragraph, the reviewer's tone changes; he is much less enthusiastic about Kean's performances. After being full of praise for his role as Richard II, and acknowledging his versatility in his role of the baron, he admits that Mr Kean's speech-making is 'indifferent' and says that his speaking powers 'laboured under considerable obscuration', meaning they were confusing and hard to understand. He goes on to describe what Mr Kean said as 'nonsense' which he believes is not worth the effort of repeating. This final sentence is very dismissive of Mr Kean's skills, in contrast to his high praise of his acting skills. This attitude is reflected in the shorter sentence construction, which rather briskly brings the review to an end.